THE BOOK OF
BRUNDALL & BRAYDESTON
A Tale of Two Norfolk Parishes

BRUNDALL LOCAL HISTORY GROUP

HALSGROVE

First published in Great Britain in 2007

British Library Cataloguing-in-Publication Data.
A CIP record for this title is available from the British Library.

ISBN 978 1 84114 630 0

HALSGROVE

Halsgrove House
Bagley Green, Wellington
Somerset TA21 9PZ
T: 01823 653777
F: 01823 216796
Email: sales@halsgrove.com
Website: www.halsgrove.com

Title page photograph: A typical scene on the River Yare at Brundall, 2006

Printed and bound in Great Britain by CPI Antony Rowe Ltd, Chippenham.

Foreword

Someone once said to me on the radio that Norfolk is just a big village. Perhaps it's the ultimate compliment for a county that likes what it is and is rather pleased that so many people want to live within its boundaries. Or perhaps it's because Norfolk has so many small communities, happy in their village identities.

As our life moves faster, with computers, PIN numbers, emails and remote call-centres making everything more impersonal, is it any wonder we like living in our villages and take a pride in what they are now and, ever more so, in what they once were?

As a resident of Brundall in the recent past (and I'm not very far away now) I know I took a growing interest in the buildings, as well as in the social history, of the village and the wider parishes. I took my children to Brundall School, wandered down to the railway station and strolled up and down The Street wondering who once lived there and what that building was used for. Progress and expansion are inevitable, so it makes wallowing in our recent history even more special.

Of course a well-written text can tell a story, but what makes this book come alive are the people of Brundall and Braydeston, past and present, looking back at us from each page through the wonderful photographs. Their faces, their smiles and fashions tell us more about our village than any social historian could.

Pleased as I am to be asked to write the foreword, please don't spend any more time on this page, just get on with the book. You won't be able to put it down!

David Clayton
BBC Radio Norfolk
2007

From Stone-Age man to modern day
How many lives have passed this way?

Who worshipped in our churches fair
In humble praise and heartfelt prayer?

Who watched it grow and soon expand
When railways came throughout the land?

Who rested in the gardens bright
'Neath heat of day and cool of night?

Who walked beside the gentle Yare
Or earned a living working there?

WE have lived here and many more
We've made our mark since days of yore.

At work all day we've done our best
And chosen things to do at rest.

These mellowed bricks, the wood, the stone
Could all tell tales of lives now gone.

Six thousand years and more to come
This lovely village has been home.

We hold it dear, remember well
Our lives spent in

Burn-in-the-Dell

© Doreen Oliver

CONTENTS

productive until the floods of August 1912, when it became waterlogged and choked with debris. In 2007 numerous boatyards occupy this area, which is still prone to flooding.

Before the Reform Act of 1832 the right to vote in an election was restricted to those owning the freehold to property with an annual value of 40s. It was publicly known how anyone voted, as poll books were printed after the election. Seats were rarely contested, and in Brundall this happened just four times during the eighteenth century – in 1702, 1714, 1734 and 1768. Poll books show that in 1702 John Kippen voted in Brundall and Richard Dawling and John Oxsmyth in Braydeston. In 1714 Richard Dawling voted in Brundall and both John and Robert Cotton in Braydeston. Nobody was eligible to vote in Brundall in 1734, but in Braydeston, again, a vote was cast by Robert Cotton and also by Thomas Burrows, and in 1768 the rector, John Gogill, voted in Brundall and William Hurnard and Edward Dammis voted in Braydeston.

The early nineteenth century produced no further eligible men to vote, as in Brundall in 1802 there were only three – Elisha de Hague (gent.), John Glaseby and Henry Harper (farmer), and only Richard Baldwin (farmer) in Braydeston. In 1806 only Henry Harper in Brundall and John Deare from Braydeston cast votes, and in 1817 Richard Gillett and Charles Prescott voted in Brundall and Robert Doe and Daniel Read in Braydeston.

Early directories show that Braydeston, with 160 inhabitants, was twice the size of Brundall, with 80. In 1836 the main landowners in Braydeston were Thomas G. Tuck, E. Walpole, Daniel Read and J. Josselyn (who had the gift of the church), while the rector was the Revd E.S. Whitbread. Sarah Bailey was the licensed victualler at the White Horse, John Cory was a shoemaker, William Lawes a shopkeeper,

Daniel Read a corn and coal merchant and James Smith a blacksmith. In Brundall the lord of the manor was Thomas Tuck and Lambert Blackwell Foster was listed as gent. The rector was the Revd Charles Penrice and Edward Cock was licensed victualler of the Ram. John Benstead Bugg was a cabinetmaker and Richard Shank Gillett a seed merchant of Hillcrest. James Glasspoole was a brick maker.

In 1845 Thomas Tuck lived in the newly built Strumpshaw Hall, T.W. Gilbert lived in Braydeston Hall and Sarah Agas was the licensed victualler at the White Horse, while in Brundall seed merchant Richard Gillett was no longer at Hillcrest. This was owned by Robert Cubitt, while William Harper was at the Ram with John Harper, a wheelwright. In 1854 James Chapman is listed as shoemaker and parish clerk in Brundall and Mary Chapman as shopkeeper of Braydeston. William Charles Miller is shown as a land agent and John Postle as a coal merchant.

The population of Brundall and Braydeston rose and fell over the years. In Domesday (1086) Brundall had 90 inhabitants and Braydeston had the same. The Black Death of 1349 may have taken many lives, although there is no evidence of this, but by the census of 1851 there were 80 people in Brundall and 160 in Braydeston.

By 1891 the parishes had merged and there was a total of 347 inhabitants, a figure that had almost doubled by 1921 due to the large amount of new housing in the village. At the time of writing the population is about 5,000.

The village has been shaped by all these people – late-Stone Age, Bronze-Age, Roman, Saxon and medieval landowners and tradesmen. So come with us now; walk through the streets, admire the old houses, rest awhile in our churches – read of the memories of Brundall's present population and enjoy.

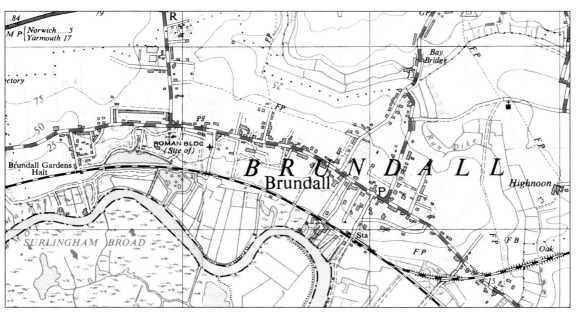

Ordnance Survey map, 1956.

A lithograph by John Berney Ladbrooke of Braydeston Church, 1828. (NORWICH CASTLE MUSEUM AND ART GALLERY)

A copy by Elizabeth Turner Palgrave, 1810, of an original drawing of 'Brundall Chapel' (St Clements) by John Deere. (NORWICH CASTLE MUSEUM AND ART GALLERY)

CHAPTER 2

Who Worshipped in Our Churches Fair
In Humble Praise and Heartfelt Prayer?

Churches and Chapels

The Church of St Michael and All Angels, Braydeston
Ann-Marie Simpson

The Church of St Michael and All Angels, Braydeston, stands alone on Braydeston Hills, its small enclosed churchyard surrounded by fields gently sloping north to Blofield and south to Strumpshaw and Brundall. This modest building is well known to hikers and dog-walkers using the village footpaths, as well as to those who attend its weekly services. The only access by car is along winding country lanes.

It is not certain why the church is so isolated from the inhabited part of Braydeston parish, although this area would have looked very different in earlier times. Lackford Run, a tributary of the Yare, was much wider and deeper than it is now, and was able to support fishing nets and water mills, and no doubt the medieval village of Braydeston was much closer to the church than modern-day housing suggests. There is no definite evidence that the village was deserted as a result of the Black Death of 1349; it may have been due to the silting up of Lackford Run, or to other changes in land use.

A church at Braydeston, is mentioned in the Domesday Book of 1086 and almost certainly stood on the current site. As with most parish churches, the original building has been altered and repaired many times over the centuries. It appears that the church once had a small chapel on its south side, the only remaining evidence being some arcading which can be seen from inside the church. Before the Reformation in the sixteenth century, the interior of the church would have been very colourful, with walls and woodwork painted in bright colours with Biblical scenes, to inspire and teach parishioners.

Today it has a more simple beauty, its high walls and large windows giving a great sense of space and light. The austerity of its plain white walls is relieved by the beautiful stained-glass window at the east end of the church. This was installed in around 1921 as a memorial to William Beck, Arthur Cole, Charles Mason and Walter Meire – parishioners who lost their lives in the First World War – and depicts the figures of Faith, Hope and Charity.

There are a number of other points of interest inside the church. At the back, beneath the tower, is a very rare stone fireplace with flue which, it is thought, was used to bake the sacred wafers for use in Holy Communion. The tower itself dates from the mid-fifteenth century and contains the one remaining bell of the three donated at that time by one William Palmer of Norwich. His name appears on the bell, along with the following rhyming Latin inscription: 'Haec fit scorum, campa laude bonorum' [sic] ('This bell was made to praise the good saints').

In the chancel can be found a rare type of stone shelf on an arched bracket, a small stone bowl for the ceremonial washing of hands and, against the south wall, a stone seat for the use of the priest. The triple stone pillar here is thought to date from the thirteenth century and may have been another entrance into the chapel, which has now disappeared. The wooden screen between the nave and the chancel, restored in 1924, has some re-set medieval wooden tracery along the top. In 1489, Robert Palmer left six marks for a new 'perke', or screen, and this may date from that time.

The nave is a good example of how the church has been altered over the centuries. On the south side

Interior of the church of St Michael and All Angels, Braydeston.

CHAPTER 3

Who Watched It Grow and Soon Expand When Railways Came Throughout the Land?

The Railway
Susen Turner

Brundall residents numbered only 63 in the entry for *White's Directory* of 1836, and yet they voiced strong objections to the proposed plan of having a railway running parallel to the main road!

Gathering momentum from the success of other railways being built around the country, a plan had been put forward to link London with Norwich and Yarmouth via Colchester and Ipswich. The Grand Eastern Counties Railway issued their proposals in 1834 and encountered endless difficulties. Once objections had been overcome, a plan to satisfy all interested parties was finalised and royal assent was received on 4 July 1836 authorising construction of the Eastern Counties Railway. Though the 'Grand' had been dropped, work was started from the London end of the line in 1837, though forced to stop at Colchester due to financial difficulties.

Norfolk residents voiced their huge disappointment and an alternative plan, put forward by the Stephensons, George and Robert, to link Norwich and Yarmouth, was adopted and royal assent was

given for Norfolk's first railway line to be built. The Act, passed on 18 June 1842, confirmed the capital at £150,000, with a loan of £50,000 for engines, carriages and other equipment. Although the original plan was far more practical, the railway company was compelled to site their track on the low ground along the river valley, where it was out of sight – the residents of Brundall had been successful in keeping it away from the road.

Construction started on 20 April 1843 at Postwick Hall Farm. The route largely followed the River Yare, with one diversion to allow for the river meandering northwards at Thorpe St Andrew, where the road and village were built at the foot of a hill, leaving insufficient room for the new railway. A cut was made across the Whitlingham Marshes and the line built on what had been the south bank for a short distance, the old river bed becoming a backwater.

The official opening of the line in 1844 was a gala day. There were 200 guests on the train, which travelled to Yarmouth in just over 55 minutes and took only 44 minutes for the return journey to Norwich. The passengers were entertained en route by Howlett's brass band, who played in the open, seat-

Brundall Station, c.1915. A goods steam train – T26 class No.490 – is met by stationmaster William Miles and staff.

Staff at Brundall Station, c. 1915. Left to right, back row: *Arthur Wright (porter), Mr Groves, Mr F. Ranson, Bertie Brinded;* front row: *Mr Brigham (signalman), William Miles (stationmaster), Mr Reddit (chief porter).*

Lad porter Bertie Brinded is poised on the ladder at Brundall Station in this photograph by W. Webb, c.1915. Note the track in the background, which led to the Coldham Hall Ferry landing-stage.

less third-class carriage next to the engine. A celebratory dinner was held that evening in the Assembly Rooms in Norwich. On the following day 1,015 passengers paid their fares to sample the first railway in Norfolk.

There were four trains each way, the fares for this service being 3s.6d. for first class, 2s.6d. for second class and 1s.3d. for third class. Cheap day returns could be had for 5s., 4s. and 2s.

The growth of traffic on the main line from Yarmouth led to the decision to build a more direct relief line from Brundall, passing through Acle and on to Yarmouth. This was a slightly shorter route, reducing the distance from Norwich to Yarmouth by two miles, which relieved pressure on the busy line and, in 1884, made Brundall a junction station.

Station Life

Five locomotives built by Robert Stephenson were in use on the original line – a 2–4–0 tender engine and four 2–2–2 tender engines. Wright of London supplied 15 coaches, 14 of which had been used for the opening ceremony.

A Cooke & Wheatstone electric telegraph system controlled the trains. The double-needle instrument workings were the first of their type, a pioneering method in advance of anything else in use at the time. The system could also be used by the public for sending urgent messages at a cost of 4s.6d. Signalling was extremely basic and consisted of a red-painted basket attached to a long pole at the end of each platform. When the basket was pulled up to the top of the pole, the train was to stop!

The station had staggered platforms with a connecting footbridge. In approximately 1860 a wooden shelter with built-in seating was provided for the use of passengers. A signal box and interlocking was provided when the line from Whitlingham Junction was doubled in 1875. The stationmaster's house contained the booking office and hall and waiting-rooms on the ground floor. There was some domestic accommodation at the rear, whilst the stationmaster and his family had use of the spacious upper floor.

The first man in charge at Brundall Station is thought to have been George W. Wilby, described in

'Ticket to ride' pre-1922, 11 September.

(GRAHAM KENWORTHY)

the 1851 census as 'railway clerk', who occupied the station house. The first mention of an official stationmaster is of Mr Charles Dearne, who held the post from 1854 to 1861. The Brundall stationmasters in post from 1850 to 1965 were as follows:

George W Wilby	*in post 1850–51*
Charles Dearne	*in post 1854–61*
Henry Lawrence	*in post 1863–65*
William Platford	*in post 1868–75*
Joseph Butters	*1875–77*
James Hall	*in post 1879*
James Hoare	*in post 1881*
Charles H. Smith	*1882–83*
Arthur J. Mann	*1883–88*
John Coker	*1888–92*
Arthur Blanden	*in post 1896*
William F. Miles	*1897 (retired 1915)*
Stephen J. Rowbury	*1915–23*
Frederick W. Wright	*1924 (retired 1929)*
R. Laurie	*1929–30*
H.A. Havers	*1930–37*
S. Hills	*1937–46*
C.E. Ward	*1946 (retired 1963)*
Leslie Sewell	*1963–65*

The dates prefixed 'in post' are from relevant directories and are an approximation, as many directories were not published every year. The other dates have been taken from staff records and so are precise. Relief stationmasters possibly covered minor gaps.

The census of 1881 shows stationmaster James Hoare and his wife Mary living at the station house with their three children. Alfred Sparrow, a signalman, lived with his wife Emma and their two children at No. 3 Station Cottage. Signalman George Mace, who was unmarried, was living at No. 8 Brundall Street with relatives. Railway porter Frederick Roll, who was only 17, and railway clerk John Carter, are also shown. The census shows five-platelayers working on the railway – William Beck, Matthew Bacon, Samuel Smith, Robert Glasspoole and William Smith, all living in Brundall.

The stationmaster at Brundall probably took responsibility for Brundall Gardens Halt, from its opening in 1924 until the post of stationmaster was discontinued there in about 1966. From 1966 onwards, a centralised station manager (later called area manager) effected management of the Brundall stations. The station was unstaffed from 1967.

The Great Eastern Railway directors' meeting of September 1882 reported that fares on several routes would be reduced and that a local train would run between Norwich and Yarmouth via Acle in each direction once an hour from 8a.m. to 8p.m. daily except Sunday. In 1884 the minutes recorded the approval of work for a coal store in the station porters' room costing £40. In 1886 the addition of a wash house and range to the stationmaster's house

Dr Beverley, Mr Edward Corder and Dick boating on the lake c.1910. (Dr Brenda Akeroyd)

View over the lake c.1910.

(Dr Brenda Akeroyd)

The pottery museum by the lake, Brundall Gardens c.1910.

Inside the pottery museum c.1910. (DR BRENDA AKEROYD)

gardens. Often he would host a garden party for the BMA, his guests enjoying the tranquil surroundings.

He had dreams of using the mere as a fish hatchery – it was certainly well stocked with trout, and many a competition was held here in later years. The site of the possible Roman dock became tiered ponds with rare pink, white and yellow water-lilies from France. There was a rock garden planted with alpines, as well as fountains, pools bordered by weeping willows and a wishing well. In another area there was a rose garden and yet another was planted with heathers. There were pampas grasses, bamboos, yuccas, blackthorns, cytisus, japonicas,

spireas, gunneras, delphiniums, peonies, snowy mespilus, *Rhus cotinus*, azaleas, rhododendrons, hellebores and bulbs everywhere, providing colour throughout the year. Dr Beverley had a good friend in Edward Corder, of Brundall, who was also a keen botanist, and they would often exchange plants. However, many of his plants were found on trips abroad to medical congresses. As his wife's health wasn't good he would often be accompanied on these occasions by his daughter, Edith, who would sketch while he worked. It was, however, in the planting of trees that Dr Beverley was particularly far seeing, creating projects in the knowledge that he would never see them reach maturity. He planted a golden oak, thought to be one of only three in the UK at the time, along with weeping ash, elms and coniferous trees of various kinds. There were Japanese maples, palms, cedars, beeches, redwoods, acers, Spanish chestnuts, tulip trees and Judas trees. Amongst these the bird life flourished and nesting boxes were provided. The varieties of birds included wrens, warblers, owls, doves, flycatchers, nightingales, woodpeckers and kingfishers. Dr Beverley introduced black swans to the mere, and on the southern side of the railway, in the marshy area, wild-fowl thrived – mallard, coot, grebe, snipe, geese, heron and migrant birds. Grass paths were created, forming walks to the river, and a boathouse provided endless fun for family and friends. In the summer

Dr Beverley's log cabin. (Dr Brenda Akeroyd)

Redclyffe House, which replaced the log cabin.

Redcliffe House in 2006. (Catherine Robson BA Hons)

there were boating parties and strawberry teas and in the winter the mere often froze over and attracted skaters. The cottages dotted about, which formerly housed marshmen, were used as summerhouses and picnic places, and one was converted into a museum to display the pottery dug from the gardens. The whole combined to provide wonder to the eye and pleasure to all.

When Dr Beverley retired from the Norfolk and Norwich Hospital, he moved to Scole, near Diss, with his ailing wife and two unmarried daughters, and, following his wife's death in 1918, the family moved to their cottage in Overstrand. Although small parcels of land on the edge of the estate were sold off to different Norwich businessmen, in 1919 Frederick Holmes-Cooper bought the rest and the gardens continued to thrive.

Frederick Holmes-Cooper, a cinema magnate, was chairman and director of Electric Theatre Ltd. Though small in stature, he had immense drive, and

The annual Yare Navigation Race, held in September, starts at Coldham Hall. Competitors set off at 15-minute intervals and sail the length of the Yare to Breydon water and back. Note the entrance to Brundall Bay Marina and Hobro's Dyke. Surlingham Broad is at the top of the photograph. (Mike Page)

Alan Savory, in *Norfolk Fowler*, explained how Charlie used to cut a piece out of the tail of every small pike he caught before he threw it back. One 25-pounder bearing the distinctive notches was showcased in The Yare pub.

Surely one of the greatest pleasures is getting a boat out on the river, and over the years such Brundall boatyards as Bell Boats, Broom, Bees Boats, Fencraft, Alpha Craft, Silverline and Buccaneer Boats, to name but a few, have hired out self-drive boats on a daily or weekly basis. Ironically, most holidaymakers tend to spend little time in Brundall waters, and explore other parts of the Broads, but for celebrities seeking peace and tranquility a holiday on the Broads can provide a cloak of anonymity. This is not always the case, however. John Stableford:

We spent a summer holiday on a Broom Admiral 8 berth cruiser and met Cliff Richards cruising on the Broads with his party and chatted about how beautiful the landscape and wildlife was in the 1960s.

One can only imagine what it was like to cruise on the Broads in the nineteenth century. In the Colman Collection in the Norfolk Heritage Centre a delightful account entitled *A Week on the Broads: August 1883*, written by six members of a Manchester rowing club,

Wherries on the Yare, c.1890. Trading wherries were often converted in the summer months for pleasure use or, permanently, as pleasure wherries. (Ffiske Family Archive)

41

'Here we are at last at our resting place, near by the huge, smart, Tea Room, where a couple of hundred persons may sit down to lunch: and later, when the place is cleared , dance mazy waltzes on the beautiful floor.'
(Arthur Patterson writing in Brundall on the Broads: An Ideal River Trip, *c.1925*

The SS Victorious, *operated by the Brundall Gardens Steamship Co. between Southtown, Great Yarmouth and Brundall Gardens, c.1925.*

John Cooper in his punt, which he built himself, c.1967.

provides an insight into a Victorian sailing holiday from Brundall:

We wrote to Mr Flowers of Brundall and engaged The Warrior... We soon arrived at Brundall and at the station were met by Fred, who was to be our head cook and bottle-washer... The week before we sailed he had been out with four clergymen and was highly commended by them for his piety but we didn't see any of this on the trip...

There was drawn up a code of rules to be followed on board:

Pianos must not be practised for more than four hours per day;
white kid gloves to be worn while swabbing the decks, thread are not considered good form; all umbrellas should be of silk.

At Breydon Water we got through all right, but some doctors ran one of the Brundall yachts aground and had to pay some wherries a cool half sovereign to tow them off... After bidding goodbye to Fred and Fawcett (the manager of the boating station) we steamed away, craning our necks out of the carriage window to catch a last glimpse of the flag of The Warrior.

Between the world wars, Brundall Gardens was a popular attraction for those visiting Brundall by pleasure steamer from Norwich and Great Yarmouth. Arthur Patterson, in a booklet published by the Brundall Gardens Steamship Co. Ltd, describes 'An Ideal River Trip on the *Victorious* from Great Yarmouth to the landing stage at the Gardens.' A

John (Jack) Golland, Commodore of the Brundall Motor Yacht Club in 1985 and 1986. Jack is remembered for organising training courses for club members for many years.

map helped the visitors to explore the gardens. Patterson described the trip as 'combining a Broadland river trip with the pleasure of spending three hours in a sylvan retreat of exquisite beauty.' The motor launch *Doris* also made trips from Foundry Bridge, Norwich. Much later on, the *Regal Lady* would bring parties to Brundall from Norwich.

Colin Chapman expressed an interest in buying the Bell/Buxton business and, when a deal was finalised in July 1971, Vic leased him the Bell/Buxton workshops, office blocks and some surrounding land.

Aquabell Ltd, formed in 1973 to produce the Aquabell 27 and the new Aquabell 33 version, went on to produce many versions of the two models, including pilot cutters (three of which still operate out of the Great Yarmouth/Gorleston pilot station), survey craft, police launches and port authority craftm etc., until 1997, when the Aquabell 33 mould tools were sold to Goodchild Marine Services at Burgh Castle. These craft were also produced under licence in Iceland and Canada.

Colin Chapman's Moonraker companies, JCL Marine and Moonraker Marine, went into voluntary liquidation on 31 October 1980. When the administrators failed to sell the company business as a going concern, it was eventually wound up and Vic re-purchased the lease with effect from 1 January 1982.

During these Moonraker years, from 1971 to 1980, Bell Boats continued to operate their Norfolk Broads holiday fleet, including day-boat hire and holiday homes. The day-to-day running of the company was under the control of Vic's brother, Arthur Bell. After the death of Vic's father, Gordon, in 1976, Arthur left the company to pursue his own interests and Vic returned to the helm of Bell Boats. Vic's son, John, joined the company in 1976 and at the time of writing is in charge of the business.

Riverscourt was sold and Vic and his wife moved into their bungalow opposite what would later be the site of the Brundall Health Clinic.

C.J. Broom & Sons Ltd

The early boating catalogues of the family business of C.J. Broom & Sons declared 'Broom's Boats are Best' next to the firm's iconic star-and-crescent pennant. This has been no idle claim, and for over 100 years in Brundall Broom's have been building boats ranging from traditional broads yachts to the ocean-going power-boats of today. Broom's boatyard is situated at the bottom of Station Road over the railway crossing. The extensive premises stretch beyond the length of the railway platform and are bounded by the Riverside Estate road on one side and upriver by the Riverside Chandlery and Bell Boats. A visitor to the modern office is likely to be met by Jennifer Broom, wife of chairman Martin Broom, or by their daughter, Amanda. Martin Broom keeps his hand on the helm from this building.

Martin Broom's grandfather, Charles John Broom, the founder of the business, was born in Blofield in 1862. He was the second child of John Broom, a coachman to T.W. Gilbert of Braydeston Hall, and Mary Ann Broom. Charles J. Broom worked for the Norfolk Broads Yachting Co., which had acquired the

The founder of Brooms Boats, Charles John Broom, with his wife, Elizabeth (Bessie) Bell Broom, c.1900.

established Brundall boatyard of George Mollet. As a craftsman he worked on constructing a variety of yachts and boats in the company's fleet until the opportunity came to manage the boatyard and eventually to acquire it and trade in his own name. To gain access to the yard at the bottom of Staithe Lane it was necessary to ring a bell for a porter to open the railway crossing. Martin Broom outlines the early days:

He was then building sailing boats for the Broads for a hire fleet and private owners. This went on in a small way until the First World War, when the yard was closed down. It was opened up again in the twenties and run by his three sons one of whom was my father.

The three sons were Charles Louis Broom (born 1892), Bernard (Barney) John Broom (born 1897) and Martin's father, Basil Christopher Broom (born 1900). By 1920 the family were living in the cottage near the level crossing at the bottom of Staithe Lane.

The advent of the motorised era in the 1920s and

An advert for the Cadet class cruiser in a 1935 Broom's catalogue.

1930s brought new challenges to the industry. Converted yachts and boat hulls were fitted with engines but were often poorly equipped, noisy and difficult to manoeuvre. Over a period of years the business developed standard motor-cruisers for private sale and for hirers wanting to discover the Norfolk Broads but needing their creature comforts. The 1938 Blakes' *Norfolk Broads Holidays Afloat* catalogue included for hire a Broom 34ft 6/7 berth *Beatrice*, with an attendant, for £17.10s. per week in high season. Also available was the Broom 24ft 3/4 berth Cadet class at £12.10s (unattended). Powered by a Morris motor, the Cadet was described thus:

These really up-to-date craft represent the acme of perfection in small craft... and combines extreme manoeuvrability with clean and economical running at all speeds.

Such was the durability of the Cadet that this same description was still being used in Broom's catalogues some 25 years later.

Charles Broom, the founder, died in 1915, and his eldest son, Charles died of TB in 1934, leaving the business to be run by Barney and Basil. Between them they managed the building programme, the expanding hire fleet and the repair shops in the period up to the Second World War.

The proximity of the railway to the boatyard had obvious advantages for holidaymakers, who could step off the train and start their broads holiday straight away.

The leisure boating industry was brought abruptly to a halt with the outbreak of the Second World War. Petrol was in short supply and the Broads and waterways were a virtual no-go area as movement was restricted. This was to be a seminal moment in Broom's history. Along with other boatyards, Broom was awarded contracts by the Admiralty for the construction of all manner of auxiliary craft. This kept the yard productive, with more than 60 men working seven days a week building in

the region of 500 boats. The arrangement also kept the efficient Broom workforce together as part of the war effort. Louis Wood, who later worked for Jack Broom (the son of C.L. Broom), recalls joining the firm as a young apprentice at that time:

After I had been at Broom for a year they said I would have to be an apprentice and defer my military service because apprentices were allowed to complete their apprenticeships before being called up. It wasn't that you dodged your service. Broom was on Admiralty work, which had to be applied for. At the time I was working on traditionally built wooden boats. They were up to 36 feet – harbour launches which were heavy old clinker-built boats like big lifeboats for harbour work, rowing cutters, pinnaces, captains' runabouts and whalers. We did a lot of whalers. I remember Victor Curtis, who was the same age as me but he started at 14 so he was ahead of me on experience. I recall Laddy Watson, who had been there some time and he knew it all.

By 1940 the threat of a German invasion was sufficiently real for measures to be taken to prevent enemy seaplanes landing on the Norfolk Broads and waterways. These consisted of lining up boats from all the hire fleets in Norfolk and connecting them together to form a linear obstruction. This tactic was never tested but by the end of the war had resulted in the deterioration of the boats, many of which sank. The Broom hire fleet escaped the worst of it because their boats were used as billets for the many service personnel based in the village because of the threat of invasion. Other boats were used to patrol the river, rather like a waterborne Home Guard. Both Bernard and Basil served part time in the Royal Observer Corps based on the old golf links.

When the war ended, Broom was able to get back to normal business more quickly than other operators – the decimation of the Norfolk hire fleets was still being felt in 1947. The Blakes (Norfolk Broads Holidays) Ltd catalogue of 1947 listed over 400 craft available for hire, compared to over 600 pre-war. Of the 33 hirers listed Broom was still the only hirer from Brundall.

A well-known character was Sidney Brigham, who was the chief engineer responsible for installing the engines. He lived all his life in Brundall and his son, John, became an apprentice engineer with him. Bill Harrison recalls working under Sidney Brigham when he served a five-year apprenticeship as a marine engineer. Bill was later to become sales manager, retiring in 1997 after 50 years' service.

Barney's son, Bernard, who was also known as Barney, joined the company in 1946 after serving with the RAF in Africa and Italy. Young Barney lived at Common Chase on the Strumpshaw Road and is remembered for being a producer with Brundall Players' amateur dramatic group. The next member

Broom's employees enjoy a break on a hot June day in 1961. The Admiral class cruiser Katinka *is moored in the background. Left to right: Keith Todd, David Penny, Peter Atkins, Ken Tyler, Tony Emms, Bob Catchpole, John Lister, Reg Northfield.*

The launch of the Bella Mia, *built for motor-racing driver A.F. Rivers-Fletcher, from Broom's boatyard on 3 March 1962. Left to right, at back: John Brigham, John Lister; back row: Charlie Hodds, Bill Harrison, Sidney Brigham, Ernie Parker, Ken Tyler, Terry Moore, Michael Bishop, David Penney, Sid ?, Philip ?, Michael Barber, Bert Platten, Ben Brown; next row: Yachting correspondent (EDP), Barney Broom junr, Keith Todd, Bob Catchpole, Rodney Hardesty, Tony Emms, Arthur Grint, Tony Yaxley, Paul Payne, Andrew Stone, Ronnie Taylor, Laddie Watson, Reggie Northfield; front row: Mrs E. Chamberlin, Mrs Basil Broom, Basil Broom, Mrs Rivers-Fletcher senr, Mrs Eva Olorenshaw, John Daynes, Mrs Rivers-Fletcher, Dick Pilgrim, Mr Rivers-Fletcher, Bob Bird, Martin Broom, Raymond Jeckells; seated: Peter Atkins, dog Rory, Mrs Jean Bird, Rachael Broom.*

these, until he was called up. Gerald Stapleton also started as a young boy, and returned for many years after the war. Henry Morse died in 1938.

During the Second World War, the Morse land in Brundall was used to grow vegetables and other essential supplies. With the war over, the family were keen to replenish their nursery stock and build up the rose-growing business again.

Soon business flourished for Henry Morse & Sons. Post-war, June Brister (later Graver), who was to become a long-standing employee, joined the firm. Her father, William Brister had been head gardener at Brundall Gardens before he moved to Witton House, and in 1947 Ernest Morse persuaded June to work for him in the firm's office in Highfield Avenue. She was a valuable asset and performed a range of duties.

During the 1950s and early '60s, truck-loads of rose bushes packed in straw, a frequent sight at Brundall Station, were sent from Brundall in the early evenings to Liverpool Street Station in London and then by special delivery to Gamages and Selfridges. Others were despatched direct to Selfridges customers under the store's own label, and to branches of Woolworths all over the country. As well as roses, hedging shrubs and other flowering plants were grown – some to sell as cut flowers, others to sell as plants. Orders were received from horticultural societies and from such government bodies as the Ministries of Transport and Education, the Board of Trade and Crown Agents. The nursery produced a comprehensive catalogue to circulate to regular customers. There was also a flourishing export business – the rose plants were first taken to Eaton, where the roots were washed before they were checked by the Health Inspector and suitably packed for transit to Japan, South Africa and elsewhere.

Alongside these major customers, the cut-flower trade supplying local florists was an important part of the business, and this was Fred Morse's area. He was regularly up at five o'clock to cut flowers ready for delivery that day. Fred delivered flowers to several florists in Norwich, including Lanham's in Prince of Wales Road, Stevenson's in London Street and Aroma in Princes Street. Another feature of the business was wedding and wreath work.

Fred Morse retired in 1963 and Florence, Ernest's wife, died the same year. Shortly afterwards Ernest decided to retire too. After a short spell in a Norwich nursing home, he returned to The Knoll and employed a housekeeper, but his health continued to fail. He died in 1965 and bequeathed Westfield Mission and the running of it to his brothers, in the hope it would continue to thrive. Fred and Emma Morse continued to live in Brundall for a while but eventually moved to Eaton Rise, where other members of the family helped care for them. Ronald Tooke, grandson of Henry Morse, terminated his independent enterprise on Strumpshaw Road at about that time.

Ernest, William and Frederick Morse.

After Ernest's death, the land in Brundall was eventually used for housing. The Morse legacy still lives on in Brundall in street names such as Westfield Road, Morse Close and Nurseries Avenue.

Henry Morse & Sons originated and introduced a number of rose varieties that are registered by the International Rose Registration Authority, and some of which were named after local people – 'Dr Edward Deacon' was a hybrid tea rose introduced in 1926. Others, named after members of the Morse family, were 'Henry Morse', 'Mrs Henry Morse', 'Ernest H. Morse', 'Florence Mary Morse', 'Ronald Tooke', 'Mary Clay' and 'Betty Morse', while 'Westfield Star' and 'Westfield Beauty' were named after the nursery. Some still appear in current catalogues, while others can be traced through specialist nurseries.

Although the original structure has been replaced, the Westfield Mission stands as a fitting tribute to Henry Morse & Sons, Rose Growers of Brundall.

R. & J. Graver, Blossom Hill Nurseries, Brundall
Jackie Warnes

Ron and June Graver had their home in Highfield Avenue built in the mid-'50s and shared it with June's parents. June was still a valuable employee of Henry Morse & Sons at that time. In the mid-'60s, shortly before the Morse land in Brundall was sold for development, Ron and June Graver started their own business.

They owned land next to and behind their bungalow in Highfield Avenue and also rented land

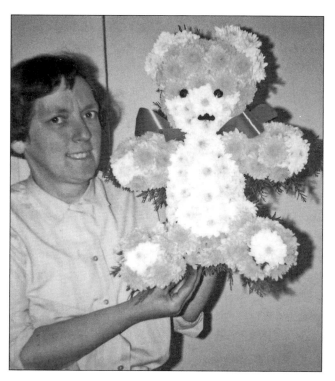

June Graver with an example of her work.

in three other locations – where the cricket ground is now, where Station New Road joins Strumpshaw Road and also land down what is now The Dales, from Broad View right down to the railway line. The land on Strumpshaw Road was rented from the ffiske family, while the land near the railway line was owned by Mr Bell of Bell Boats.

Ron and June worked full time themselves and also employed three young men – Tony Graver (Ron's nephew), Terry Boast and Malcolm Mingay.

As well as over 20,000 rose bushes, they also grew a variety of shrubs and hedging plants. They took their own cuttings from these and reared them for sale. Fruit trees were imported direct from Holland and later sold. They also grew flowers for cutting, including dahlias and chrysanthemums. Another part of the business was devoted to wedding flowers and floral funeral tributes, using some of their own flowers but also buying in others from Burlingham Agricultural Station and Jones' of Great Plumstead. June had learnt this part of the trade from Florence Morse. She remembers making floral tributes in the shape of harps with broken strings, teddy bears and children's chairs, as well as more traditional shapes. Ron made the basic shapes from wire (even wire coat-hangers sometimes), as they were unable to buy the Oasis bases widely available now. June would often work all day and until late at night on these,

and the selling price per item never exceeded £4. It was often a worry for June when wedding flower orders clashed with floral tributes ordered late and often in quantity by funeral directors.

Ron would see the customers in the office and advise them on all aspects of their orders. He was well-liked and gave reassuring advice, even though the phrase 'resting where no shadows fall' may have been used rather often!

Just before Christmas, their time was taken up making holly wreaths, which never cost more than 4s. each. Prices have changed greatly since then, but their wreaths were excellent value at the time.

By the mid-'80s, when June's father had died and her mother's health had declined to the extent that she needed a great deal of care, June and Ron were obliged to give up their business and devote their time to her. Their enterprise was much missed by local residents, who were forced to shop further afield for quality flowers and plants.

George Edward Deacon
The Hethersett Society

'Nine-ed' is a rather unusual nickname. To unravel its origin, take the letter 'G', written large and mistaken for a figure '9', followed by 'ed'... problem solved! Many were the problems deliberately faced by George Deacon. Some readers might be more familiar with his name as applied to a rose. Who was the man who was accorded such an honour? Certainly a professional man of medicine and many other talents, George Edward Deacon, born on 6 October 1863, was the eldest of four and had two brothers and a sister. His father, a practising surgeon in Hethersett, evidently encouraged his son's later distinguished career in medicine. Following education at Oundle School, Peterborough, and at Paston Grammar School, North Walsham, George qualified MRCS at St Bartholomew's in 1886. The same year he was awarded the Bentley Prize, a highly prestigious award for surgeons, and became a

Licentiate of the Society of Apothecaries in 1887.

Dr Deacon returned to Norfolk to work, possibly occasioned by the illness of his father. He worked at the Norfolk & Norwich Hospital, held influential posts as medical referee with various insurance societies and was the surgeon to the Odd Fellows and Forester's societies for many years. There is much evidence to suggest that George worked hard to

Left: *Dr George Deacon, who retired to Deacon House, Blofield Road, Braydeston, in 1927.*

promote patient access to medical services, including his involvement with a local nursing benefit club. There was also a very adventurous side to his character – he jointly owned the first ever private motorcycle in Norfolk.

His main contribution to Braydeston culture was his interest in plants and creepy crawlies. His study of the fungi and diseases affecting roses led to his joining the Mycological Society and his founding of the Hethersett Horticultural Society. In retirement he became a prominent member of the National Rose Society and won their coveted Dean Hole Medal. His interest saw him judging for the Norwich & Norfolk Horticultural Society and donating a cup for roses. His friendship with Ted Ellis and with the ever-increasing number of horticulturalists in the area deepened amid great mutual admiration and respect.

Although George Deacon died, aged 95, in November 1958, his name lives on in Deacon Close, Brundall. And for those wishing to savour his rose, it is available, at the time of writing, from Messrs Peter Beales at Attleborough, listed as Dr Edward Deacon.

Ted Ellis
Golda Conneely

In the winter of 1943 the well-known Norfolk naturalist Ted Ellis moved to Brundall with his wife, Phyllis, and their young son, John. They had been living in various lodgings since their first home, in Martineau Lane, Norwich, was bombed in June 1942.

It seems possible that Ted's friendship with Dr Deacon led the family to the village, where they took the small house Kilnhurst on Blofield Road, overlooking Braydeston Hills. It was a wonderful hunting ground for Ted and three-year old John, and for the many visitors who were always seeking Ted out, and who sometimes stayed in the rather chaotic

In 1943 Ted Ellis moved to this semi-detached house (on the right) on Blofield Road.

house. Visitors would come in through the back door, which opened straight into a crowded kitchen containing a full-sized bath, a sink, a copper, drying washing, small children, and Phyllis, trying to cook over an open fire.

Their daughter Mary was born in Brundall in June 1944, and their son Martin just before Christmas 1945. Ted was working at the Castle Museum in Norwich, and kept up a huge amount of correspondence with his many scientific friends, including Norfolk-born botanist Arthur Mayfield.

In 1945 Wheatfen, the cottages and 150 acres of fen at Surlingham were offered to the Ellises as their permanent home – and lifetime's work. Days before they signed the lease Ted was offered a job at the Mycological Institute in London, but he and Phyllis knew where they wanted to be, and they left Brundall for Surlingham in January 1946.

The contribution Ted Ellis made to natural history is immeasurable. Many children learned their love of nature through Ted and his boundless enthusiasm.

Elsie Butcher
of Ye Olde Smithy Tea Rooms
Jackie Warnes

Elsie Butcher was born in Barrack Street, Norwich, on 28 July 1895, the fourth child of John and Elizabeth Rudduck. Her parents both came from Suffolk but moved to Norwich about 1892/93 with their ever-increasing young family. In the census of 1891 John Rudduck was shown as a coal hawker and in 1901 was described as a self-employed hawker. Whether he sold from a horse and cart or had premises is not known, but perhaps Elsie inherited her flair for business from her father. It has been said that Elsie had a business in Norwich before she ever came to Brundall, though no evidence has been found to support this.

In 1918 Elsie married Walter Butcher, but the marriage was short and unhappy. At the time she applied for a licence to marry at the Primitive Methodist Chapel, Dereham Road, Norwich, she described herself as a labeller in a brewery. Walter soon deserted Elsie, leaving her to support herself. She kept her married name but reverted to the title of 'Miss', and it was as 'Miss Butcher' she was known in Brundall, although her family and close friends called her 'Ginger'. As a lady on her own, she certainly made an excellent job of supporting herself.

Arriving in Brundall in the early 1930s, Elsie initially worked for Mr Drake, who owned a shop on The Street. When Mr Drake retired, Elsie took over the business, possibly with some financial help from Jimmy Childs.

Jimmy, a friend of Elsie's, the milkman in Limpenhoe, owned an open truck which was often in great demand. Margaret Shingles thinks he also farmed some land at Strumpshaw.

A recent photo of the Revd Canon Pat Atkinson on her travels.

Much of the money for all these schemes has been raised quietly and consistently by the people of Norfolk, many of whom have been spurred into action after hearing Pat's story and seeing her heart-rending pictures. Pat discovered that the problems she faced in South India could not be solved by money alone – she needed to win the trust of the children and families and to understand their culture before she could improve their lives.

During her visits to India she stays in very humble surroundings, risking her life in appalling conditions with little food. She is supported at home by her family and many friends, who pray for her safety and welfare so that she is able to do the work God has called her to do.

As the projects have developed, Pat has been able to organise trips to India for her supporters so that Norfolk people can see for themselves how the money raised is being used. Pat has extended her work in Trivandrum, and plans to buy land on which to build a school which will house a boys' home, a girls' home, an office, a meeting-hall and office facilities. She is working with local churches in South India to help some of the neediest children there and, in Sri Lanka, is also helping Father Terence build a community centre for his parish.

Sri Lanka faces a lot of problems following the Tsunami in 2005 and many people are starving. Her tireless endeavour for the poorest people in India and Sri Lanka is an inspiration to us all. Pat stresses that this work could not happen without the continuing financial and spiritual support that has been behind it since its conception.

We were overjoyed when the 2007 New Year

Honours list included an MBE awarded for her services to street children and to the impoverished people of South India. It was in the the *Eastern Daily Press* that most of us read the announcement, which was followed by words so typical of Pat:

I don't like publicity. We don't work that way. This MBE isn't about me at all, it's about the people of Norfolk who have supported us for the past 16 years. They have stood by us when things have been really difficult. I'm just an ordinary person, but I fell in love with some kids – that's what did it – love.

Mike Snowling
Robin Middleton

At the time of writing Mike Snowling is recovering from a bout of the hard work which he loves and adores and possibly could scarcely do without – charity work for the benefit of children. On this occasion it happens to be involvement with the children of Chernobyl. With this, his patronage of the 'Golden Sovereigns' display troupe, his support of the Girl Guides, his work as chairman of the Broadland District Council and his involvement with countless other minor matters, he says he is busier in retirement than in his 25 years of running Shiels Court as a residential guest-house for the elderly, which he sold as a going concern. Shiels Court has always represented home for Mike and, considering his long association, it is no wonder he regards it in this way.

Mike was born at Dickleburgh, the illegitimate son of a young mother. It seems that some members of the family never forgave him for the 'shame' he brought upon their name and, after a period of great unhappiness during which he was continuously blamed for everything and anything, Michael was abandoned by his family and sent to Bramerton Lodge remand home. On one fateful occasion, when asked if he had played truant the previous day, he nodded – he didn't understand the word 'truant'. He smiles as he tells me that if they had accused him of bunking off, he would have doubtless invented some story or other, but as it was he found himself moved on. Bereft of any such luxury as pocket money, he treasured a small memento given to him by a social worker in Norwich – a photograph in a silver frame inscribed 'from your Mum, Dad and little brother'. The news of a new brother kept alive in him a curiosity about his family, despite his treatment at their hands.

He came to Brundall in the late 1940s, when Shiels Court housed some 24–25 boys under the tutelage of Mr Deasley. Their many skirmishes and exploits as they struggled through their daily existence were typical of lads who had never known what it was to live a normal family life, yet there was a solidarity among them second to none. His daily routine began with clearing up after the younger boys, stripping

Mike Snowling superimposed on one of his buses.

soiled beds, then off to the station to take the train to Whitlingam Station for Hillside Avenue School, Thorpe. Mike remembers some fun and games in the Court when he and an accomplice started playing with electrical switches so that the lights on the Christmas Tree would blink on and off and look as posh as other people's… and the time he stopped one of the junior boys getting a beating.

The Christmas tree episode evidently began a fascination with Christmas lights which was later to evolve into the yearly festival of illuminations on his bungalow in The Street.

His involvement with things electrical saw Michael later obtain an apprenticeship with the Electricity Board in King's Lynn. His electrical training extended to the wireless and, in an attempt to get a better signal, he connected the aerial to the bathroom tap. His foster carer saw this as an attempt at electrocution! On he went.

He bought a bicycle to take him to work and to technical college. In his spare time, at weekends especially, he still felt baseless, and on one occasion cycled back to his home. If he had not been shown love in Brundall, it was the place where he had at least been shown care.

Joining the Boys' Service in the Army, Mike developed his skills in electrics and wired up loudspeakers to neighbouring billets after buying himself a radio set from Snellings. With a pal he built a transmitter, and managed to jam 'Radio Luxembourg', an achievement for which he was duly reprimanded.

While serving in Borneo in the Royal Signals he combined his military service with a rekindling of his interest in the cinema and children, and spent much time and energy putting on film-shows at a Catholic children's orphanage. He had made up his mind, however, to move on from the Army, and decided to buy himself out. Determined not to go and live with his mother near Diss, he came home on Friday, 13 November 1959, to his only home. By then the Court had closed and was being refitted as an agricultural college hostel.

Looking for work as an electrician, Mike eventually secured a post at Swainsthorpe Hospital. Later working at Little Plumstead Hospital, he was encouraged to become a nurse. Once trained, though, he got itchy feet and, with Vauxhall cars recruiting in Norwich, Mike soon found himself in the Luton and Dunstable area of Bedfordshire. Finally he set up his own heating installation and maintenance business there, and married and brought up a family of four children.

In 1976 he decided to return to Norfolk, and negotiated for a property in Weston Longville. A tragic accident to the vendor prevented the sale and at the same time Mike was told that Shiels Court had come onto the market. He was anxious to acquire the property, but the Court was by then in a sad state of repair and it was over a year before Mike could return. Taking in students to help offset problems with the initial cash flow, he looked into the possibility of reopening the building as a children's home. When this proved an unviable proposition, it became a home for senior citizens.

Mike finally 'retired', and in 2007 is serving his third term as chairman of Broadland District Council. During his terms of office he has highlighted the plight of underprivileged children and has been both surprised and delighted at the response. He maintains a keen interest in planning issues and describes himself as 'the working man's councillor'. He currently lives opposite Shiels Court.

Alan James Herbert Hunter
Ann-Marie Simpson

Many of those who enjoy a good crime detection story will be familiar with Inspector Gently, whose exploits are recorded in 48 novels written over a period of 40 years by Alan Hunter. Not many, though, will realise that Alan lived in Brundall for a number of those years until his death in 2005. Like his creation, Alan was a quiet, self-effacing man. The fact that so many of the titles began with 'Gently', seems appropriate, and he was often referred to as a real gentleman.

Alan's literary connections started early. His recollection of a childhood meeting with Arthur Ransome is referred to in both *Literary Norfolk* and in an interview with the *Eastern Daily Press* in 1992. Ransome listened to the boys recounting their adventures on the Broads. Like Ransome, Alan loved the natural world and made a study of it from his earliest years. He used to keep nature notes as a child and won a book on natural history as a prize at school for a year-long study of a bird. His first published essay as a 14-year-old schoolboy, called 'Coots protecting their nests', later proved useful as reference material when he wrote articles on natural history for the *Eastern Evening News*. His first paid work was a short story about turkey poaching, published in the *Farmers Weekly*.

Alan was born in Hoveton St John, his father a poultry farmer and his uncle, Percy Hunter, a Ludham boat builder. His five sisters taught their much younger brother to sail and gave him his first boat. The sisters were quite lively, it seems – they were the first girls in that village to wear trousers and played in a local band in the 1920s and '30s. His sister Audrey, who played drums in the band, became Mrs Bennett and later moved to Brundall where, for a while, she served as president of the local WI. She first lived in St Laurence Avenue and later had a flat in Kenmare, at the junction of The Dales and The Street.

Alan helped in the business for a while when he left school, but was relieved to be able to volunteer for the Air Force at the outbreak of war, serving as an electrician. It was during the war that he met his future wife, Adelaide Cubitt, when, by chance, both of them were enjoying a visit to the Castle Museum in Norwich – Mrs Hunter recalls it was on a rainy Thursday afternoon. Her parents had moved from their business in Lowestoft to Brundall at the outbreak of war, and had bought the house called The Shrubbery. Apart from keeping bees there, Mr Cubitt later kept chickens and got supplies and advice from Alan's father. Alan and Adelaide married in 1944. After the war they settled at The Shrubbery with Adelaide's parents before moving to a bungalow on The Street, Fairwinds, built by Mr Gedge, two doors from the Ram.

For a while, Alan worked for Mr Cubitt looking after the bookshop part of the business. He then opened his own bookshop in Norwich and lived above it, and later owned a bookshop in Cromer. They moved to Brundall in the early 1960s, when Helen was born, then back to Norwich, renting out their bungalow, finally returning to Brundall in 1974, to St Laurence Avenue, where Adelaide and Helen still live in 2007.

As well as articles in the local press, Alan liked to write poetry, his first independent publication being *The Norwich Poems* (1944). While living in Norwich he also wrote a few plays, which were put on at premises in Cow Hill by Norfolk Drama Organiser Jack Mitchley. One of these featured Inspector Gently. Alan's early short stories were variously about an old Norfolk man (Southcote) who told incredible tall tales, a haunted church where a skeleton was endlessly looking for his lost bones, a goldfish that could predict sports results and so forth! He then developed the character who was to dominate his writing for the next 40 years.

As with many a successful writer, he suffered frequent disappointments in the early days. Adelaide recalls that on one occasion, presuming that a parcel in the post was yet another rejection, Alan placed it in the bottom of a cupboard without opening it. Some weeks later she suggested he should at least check the contents and he discovered that the publisher was very much interested and had only returned the material for amendment. Thus Gently was born. The first Gently story – *Gently Does It* – was published in 1955. Based at Scotland Yard, Gently finds himself solving crimes around the country and very often in places which sound very familiar to Norfolk readers, with obvious references to the Broads and Norwich. Even the name Gently was inspired by a Star class yacht built by Uffa Fox and used in Britain in the 1948 Olympics. The proceeds from the sale of this novel allowed him to buy a sailing cruiser, which he purchased for £75 at the annual Broads boat sale. Six years after the first Gently book was published, he sold his bookshop and became a full-time writer.

In the '60s there had been discussions about the possibility of making his book *Gently Go Man* into a road movie, but the cult classic *Easy Rider* came along and the project fell through! He was thrilled when, in 1995, the first Gently book was reprinted by Constable publishers. This book had been reprinted twice in 1955 and was also published in America, Italy and Denmark. Alan had hoped that Gently would eventually make it to our TV screens. In the year leading up to his death he had been approached about possible film rights, and on April 8 2007 'Gently Go Man' was aired on television. Alan would have been delighted.

His approach to writing was methodical. Each year he would spend around two months thinking out and planning a plot, then around three months typing up the book. He would work in the small extension at the back of his bungalow for about five hours each morning and then go out walking in the countryside in the afternoon. His daughter Helen recalls that on his return he would talk about things he had seen. She sometimes accompanied him on these walks.

His writing was no doubt enriched by his vast knowledge of life on the Broads. Those locals who used the Ram on Monday lunchtimes recall Alan with great affection. He was an interesting man to speak to, as he puffed on his pipe at the bar. Inspector Gently was a pipe smoker, and one of Alan's favourite reads was the Maigret books – Adelaide recalls how pleased he was when Inspector Gently was described as the English Maigret. Other favourites were Jane Austen and Arthur Ransome. After he gave up sailing, Alan bought a motor caravan in which he and his family enjoyed travelling to France and to the far north of Scotland. In an interview in the *Eastern Daily Press* in 1992 it is suggested he rediscovered there the inspiring wild

BP Trefoil Guides, 1987. Left to right, back row: *Tracy Wright, Jeannette Hall, Heather Dunseath;* front row: *Caroline Daniels, Ruth Lowrie, Sarah Dunseath, Alison Harvey.*

Brownie's outing to Bressingham, 1998. Left to right, staff: *Helen Watkins (Brown Owl), Mr Snowling;* back row: *Carly ?, Jackie Thomas, Rachael Watkins, Kylie Sutton, Caroline Silby, Astrid Barber, Rachel ?, Nichole ?;* middle row: *Carole Thailess, Katrina Haggerty, Rachel Wilkinson, Nicola Wall;* front row: *Joy ?, ?, Claire Etheridge, Leanne Heavens, ?, Melanie Cunnane, Rebecca Harrison.*

1st Brundall Rainbows, 2002. Left to right, back row: *Bobbie Sharpe, Kate Mackintosh, Afonwen and Trudy Davies;* middle row: *Fiona Lee, Rebecca Lawrence, Hannah Stevenson, Poppy George, Heidi Hogg, Sian Murray, Laura Edwards;* front row: *Charlotte Higgins, Kelly-Jane Hale, Kim Anasrasiou, Bethany Wagstaff, Sarah Andrews.*

peared in the direction of the washing facilities every time chores had to be done. The kettle, being the dirtiest piece of equipment by the end of the camp, was presented to the Guide on the last day with great ceremony! At another meeting a couple of senior Guides sent to light a portable barbecue failed to take it out of its cardboard box and it went up in smoke!

The 1st Brundall Brownie pack opened in February 1967 with Molly Cobb as Brown Owl. Subsequent Brown Owls have been Janice Tandy, Eileen Rivers, Sue Knickle, Helen Watkins and Angela Tisdale. In February 1977 the pack celebrated their 10th birthday with a presentation of the Brownie story to parents and a party.

In 1972 Rosemary Bickers opened the 2nd Brundall Brownie Pack. She was succeeded by Gill Watson, Margery Cordner, Julie Sutton, Sue Mackenzie and Sarah Bullent. Brownie meetings were designed to be a mixture of fun and education. The girls were encouraged to take badges; often the whole pack would work towards one. The leaders

used to look forward to one particular fund-raising event – a sponsored silence. What bliss!

Pack holidays were part of the programme. Both packs and various 'mad' helpers took off for a week of fun and frivolity at various locations around Norfolk. The most memorable outing was in December 2001, when over 100 girls and leaders visited Banham Zoo.

The 1st Brundall Rainbow unit opened in 1998, with Guider Sarah Bullent, and the 2nd Rainbow unit opened in 2005.

Between 1990 and 2005 three of Brundall's Guiders served as district commissioners, coordinating activities across the district. They were Margery Cordner, Diana Buck and Mary Hall.

All the units join together each year to celebrate Thinking Day, the day we think of all the other Guides. This corresponds with the joint birthday of Lord and Lady Baden-Powell, our founders. We have also celebrated other events, such as the Millennium and the Queen's Jubilee.

Youth Club visit to Great Yarmouth in the 1950s. Left to right: *Dick Geary, John Bailey, Dorothy Marshall, Rex Barrett, Elizabeth Merrison, ?.*

The Youth Club
Golda Conneely

When the Memorial Hall opened in the late 1940s one of the groups using it was called Brundall Youth Organisation. In the 1960s there was a Youth Club at the hall, and by the 1970s they were holding dances a couple of times a year. In 1973 John Larwood and Vic Collier took over the running of the Youth Club, which they did very successfully for many years, and by 1983 the discos attracted about 200 young people every other week.

When a hard-court games area was built behind the hall, 24 members of the Youth Club helped by shifting 80 tons of material with wheelbarrows. They also raised £600 for the hard-court area, and negotiated for a grant for equipment. Very successful musical evenings were held to entertain senior citizens, one of whom wrote that the young ladies behaved like airline stewardesses, and the young boys were helpful, which made John Larwood wonder if they were talking about the right Youth Club! In 2007 the Youth Club still meets at the hall on Thursday evenings.

In 2001 a young man called Craig Whitlam, determined to get a skateboard park built as part of the outdoor amenities at the Memorial Hall, raised £500 and persuaded Brundall Parish Council and Broadland District Council to provide £3,000 and £7,000 respectively. As a result of his efforts skateboarding could be enjoyed more safely and stylishly in Brundall.

Theatre in Brundall
Golda Conneely, John Thomson

TIB, as it is affectionately known, has staged live dramatic and musical performances in Brundall for over 30 years in the Memorial Hall, apart from its closure during refurbishment in 2000/2001, the hall has seen nearly 100 major TIB productions, including plays, musicals and 28 traditional pantomimes of a consistently high standard.

On 14 November 1972 a new society to be known as Theatre in Brundall was formed to follow on from the Blofield and Brundall Players. The chairman was Alan Cobb, the secretary Trixie Smith and the treasurer Michael Waters, and the steering committee included Mrs Ann Wood, Bert Wright, Mrs Pat Bell and Jeff Cox. The stated aim of the society was 'to provide entertainment in all forms'. The staple offering of one or more plays, a summer musical and a traditional pantomime each year has not changed a great deal. In its first year, TIB put on *The Queen of Hearts*, *Brush with a Body*, the Brun-Dells Pierrot Show and its first pantomime, *Robinson Crusoe*. For the desk and the other had to stand. Patients were by now more frequently using cars to visit the surgery. The front drive of Bradesfield was often full of cars and those parked on Blofield Road caused obstruction to the road traffic, leading to complaints, particularly from the bus company. A site for a health centre was identified in The Dales and after an eight-year process Brundall Health Centre opened in 1980. The rapid growth of medical provision in Brundall can be judged by the fact that by the time Dr Gray retired in 1985, the number of doctors practicing at the health centre had grown to four, Dr Rigby having moved from Acle surgery and Drs Harston and Ashman having joined the practice. The increasing size of the practice also made the joint partnership of Acle surgery and Brundall surgery very difficult to manage, and in 1997 there was a completely amicable split into two separate practices. Dr John Rigby retired in 2004 and Dr David Varvel in May 2006, both, like Dr Gray, having faithfully served the community for many years.

The Brundall practice used to have branch surgeries in both Lingwood and Cantley. This was once common to rural practices, where most patients had no transport and the doctor had to go to the patient. In Cantley, prior to 1960, the surgery was in the front room of a house rented for a few shillings a week. In about 1960 Dr Gray persuaded the Cantley Village Hall committee to let him put up a hut, to be used as a surgery, next to the Village Hall, which would then be used as the waiting-room. In Lingwood a cottage was rented in which the kitchen/bathroom was the consulting-room, the consulting couch being a board over the bath. The only souce of heating was the oven, which was switched on with the door left open!

A rural practice on the river can bring about some unusual situations. Dr. Varvel remembers being called to a sick seaman on a coaster. As it was low tide the vessel had to anchor in mid Yare and Dr Varvel had to be rowed out to the boat and climb a rope ladder to attend to the man, who could not speak a word of English. On another occasion, on Halvergate marshes, when a farm worker kicked by a heavy working horse suffered fractured ribs, a five-barred gate was taken off its hinges and used as a stretcher to carry him off the marsh to the ambulance, which could get nowhere near the patient.

New technology has greatly assisted the doctor. Dr Varvel recalls that when he first came to Brundall he was on emergency call in the Reedham area every other weekend. On completing a call he would phone his wife in Brundall, from a phone box, to see if there had been any further demands for his services during his absence. If there were none, he would drive the nine miles home to Brundall, often to find that a call had come in while he was on the road, and he would have to return to Reedham. Mobile phones certainly help nowadays. Within the surgery docu-

ments and records are now electronically stored and, with a computer in each consulting room, consultations in 2007 can be carried out in a virtually paper-free environment.

Sue Barrett, who started with the practice in 1969 helping with the administration, is still working for the practice and has taken part in all the developments since. When she started at Bradesfield, she remembers, there was herself, assisting with the administration and dispensing, another lady who worked in the afternoons to cover the phones and do the typing, and the two doctors. In 2007, as well as the doctors, there are 20 other practice staff, including secretaries/receptionists, dispensers, nurses and care assistants. Through the Health Centre patients have access to services including those of community midwives, community nurses, occupational therapists, speech therapists, physiotherapists and dieticians.

Just 50 years ago patients were still in the habit of calling out the doctor only when absolutely necessary, and a patient with appendicitis once cycled to the surgery for treatment! In 1969 the Brundall practice had 1,500 patients on its list; in 2007 it has 8,500, and is a modern Health Centre run by staff dedicated to achieving and maintaining a quality health service designed to meet the needs of its patients.

We are also lucky to have the dental surgery, which has served the village for over 25 years. Opened on 3 November 1980 by John Wade in what was then his home at No. 114 The Street, Brundall, the surgery is still there in 2007, as is John, although expansion of the practice has meant that it is no longer his home.

Creative and artistic are words which only begin to describe the following organisations.

Brundall Flower Club
Pat Thomas

Following flower-arranging classes run by Norfolk County Council, Brundall Flower Club was formed in 1973. At that time Mrs Joyce Wright, a national judge and demonstrator for the National Association of Flower Arrangement Societies (NAFAS) lived in Brundall, and we were very fortunate to have her guidance in forming a flower club. The inaugural meeting, held on 13 September 1973, was followed by monthly meetings.

The first flower festival, arranged by the club at Brundall Church in the same month, was entitled 'Harvest Glory'. There was an annual exhibition for the next three years – 'Brundall Life', 'From Your Bookshelf' and 'Moments in History', all held in the Memorial Hall. To mark the Queen's silver jubilee in 1977, the club had permission from British Rail to clear the gardens on Brundall Station and plant up the beds in red, white and blue. Every evening saw

Brundall Flower Club's first flower festival, 'Harvest Glory', was held in St Laurence Church in September 1973.

SATURDAY 23rd MAY

BRUNDALL CARNIVAL DAY

(In aid of the Hall Rebuilding Fund)

1.30 FANCY DRESS COMPETITION FOR CHILDREN outside Springdale Old Peoples Home (no entry fee)

1.45 **PROCESSION Through Village to HALL GROUND**
Decorated Vehicles — Two Bands

2.30 Official Opening of the Fete by :-
OLIVIA BREEZE
('Goldilocks' from this years Theatre Royal Pantomime)

DONKEY DERBY - **PUNCH & JUDY** - **DISPLAYS**

DEMONSTRATIONS - **TOMBOLA**

Many prizes including :-
STAR PRIZE FREE WEEKS HIRE OF THE 6 BERTH LUXURY CRUISER "PAMELEENA BEE"
(given by Mr. & Mrs. Beales, Bees Boats Brundall)

PONY RIDES - **SIDE SHOWS** - **PRODUCE STALLS**

REFRESHMENTS & ICE CREAM

Other prizes to be won include :-
SEASIDE BUNGALOW HOLIDAY - 12 TEDDY BEARS
24 BOXES CHOCOLATES - DOLL WORTH £7
and 1,000 POTS OF HONEY, ETC.

Special Attraction :-
THE TEDDY BEARS PICNIC
(See Reverse for Details)

Admission : Adults 2/- Children 6d.

8.00 **CARNIVAL DAY DANCE to The Collegians**
Tickets 6/- now on sale

Programme for Carnival Day, 23 May 1970.

members carrying cans to water the little plants. The project was very successful and the club received a letter of thanks from British Rail.

In 1982 club members arranged flowers to decorate the exhibits in the Strumpshaw Steam Museum. As a result Mrs Key, wife of Jimmy who owns the Museum, presented the club with a rose bowl to be awarded in club competitions.

Over the years the club has donated money to many local charities, the most satisfying donation being the £1,000 raised to buy Abigail, a golden labrador, for the RNIB. Mr Ken Gooch, a Norwich man with a beautiful black labrador guide dog, spent an evening at one of our meetings and accepted our cheque on behalf of the RNIB.

At our monthly meetings we usually welcome a demonstrator, and about once a year a practice evening is held at which members can be helped to complete a designated flower arrangement. We have had coffee mornings, many in the lovely garden at Pendle Cottage in The Street, where Brundall residents have joined us to have coffee, a sit-down and a chat after doing their shopping. Just before Christmas each year, at a Christmas fair held in the Memorial Hall, flower arrangements made by our

members are sold, and a raffle boosts our charity fund. Over the years, visits to well-known local gardens have been arranged, as well as visits to nurseries and plant centres and church flower festivals.

The last 30-plus years have been memorable in many ways, and we like to think the oft-quoted motto flower arrangers' motto, 'Fun, Friendship and Flowers', has brought many hours of pleasure.

The Cribbage League
Sinclair Simpson

The two Brundall pubs, The Yare and the Ram, play in the Broadland Cribbage League, which has been well established since at least the 1980s. The League is for pub teams in the area and trophies include two knock-out cup competitions plus pairs and singles. League matches run throughout the winter months, and twice in recent years the Ram team has had a 24-hour 'Cribathon' in aid of local charities.

There are so many groups and activities in Brundall and Braydeston that it is not possible to write about

The 'Cribathon 2006' crib charity event at the Ram public house in aid of Caister lifeboat. Left to right: A representative of Caister lifeboat, Sinclair Simpson, David Berry, Ray ?, Allan ?.

Rachel Drake and many teddy friends at the Teddy Bears' Picnic in 1970.

in 2005 the officers were keen to reunite the picture with its benefactor. Coincidentally, the crew already had links with Springdale, having offered to help with its refurbishment. They noticed a press cutting in Elspeth's scrapbook of her presenting the painting and so were able to return it to her. Elspeth was thrilled to see the painting again but would like to see it back in Navy hands eventually. Meanwhile, it remains at Springdale.

Two noticable features of the building are the roof, which is covered with copper sheeting, and the copper weathervane, which is in the form of a Roman merchant ship of the type that may have called at Brundall 1800 years ago. The name Springdale is, of course, a reference to the meaning of the name Brundall.

Arts and Crafts Architecture
Liz Waterman

At the turn of the century a fashion developed for the Arts and Crafts style of architecture. Pioneered by William Morris, Pugin and Voysey, this style of architecture was highly individual, and was inspired by the medieval and vernacular, industrial building processes being rejected in favour of simple, hand-crafted details. Minimalist design was a strong feature.

Norfolk's most famous architect from this period was George Skipper (1854–1948). Not only was he responsible for some of Norwich's notable buildings (Norwich Union's headquarters), but also for cottages and country houses, which blended with more rural surroundings.

Brundall has some fine examples of Arts and Crafts houses, although the architects are unknown. The pair on Station New Road are typically asymmetrical and individual in their design. Making use of local building skills and materials, they are thatched, and their interior wooden beams display wooden pegs to 'explain' their construction. Both houses feature wood panelling. Their fireplaces have plain brick or tile insets and, of course, were fitted with servants' bells! The windows are leaded in Arts and Crafts style. There was originally a shared well (water was not laid on until 1954) and a box-edged vegetable garden.

The houses, the first to be built on Station New Road, were completed in 1907 by Henry William Massingham (of Mayertorne Manor, Bucks) and his wife Ellen (née Snowden). The first tenants of the houses were George Elden Burrow and Mrs Mann, while No. 16 was owned from 1919 to 1944 by Mrs Jessie Fitch, a widow from Braydeston House.

Embracing the tradition of thatching, Nether House on Strumpshaw Road is also a beautiful Arts and Crafts house.

Although Marsh Acre on Strumpshaw Road is very different from the thatched houses, its shape is

Nether House.

again asymmetrical. It was probably built in the 1920s for a man called Sandys-Winch, a City Council parks and gardens expert who designed a fantastic garden which included two large herbaceous borders, tennis courts and a very large box-edged vegetable garden. Other owners over the years have included Mr C.W. Butler, who worked for Norwich Union, and Mr Wilkinson, who was manager of Curls department store (now Debenham's) in Norwich. In the 1960s some of the garden was sold off to build the neighbouring houses.

The Old Beams
(now the Lavender House)
Elizabeth Asbury

We arrived in Brundall in April 1963. The Old Beams had already been a tearoom, simply serving teas in the front room from blue and white Cornish-ware crockery on tables with check cloths. We had just sold our guest house in Overstrand and had taken out a huge private loan to secure the attractive premises. It had always been Adrian's ambition to have a restaurant and to be self-employed. The Old Beams had a pretty front garden and a lawn at the side, while the little thatched shop to the right was rented out as a lock-up for hardware supplies. To keep us solvent, Adrian worked part time teaching butchery at Norwich City College. We were young (only in our early twenties), enthusiastic, and eager to make a success of the Old Beams.

We lived above the restaurant and started alterations, knocking an entrance through to the front room that we wanted as a bar. There was an Aga in the kitchen. We bought furniture from High Wycombe, and cooking equipment, including stoves and a bain-marie, from London. We cleaned, painted and polished to create a traditional décor, and in the summer of 1963 served light lunches and teas to the few holidaymakers from the boats and holiday cottages on the River Yare.

Advertising three weeks ahead of our ambitious opening night, we took lots of bookings and stayed up most of the night before the opening. Fully

The Old Beams.

booked and feeling the strain, we served the first sitting. Then, disaster! – the power failed and that night we had to compensate with free drinks, then free meals for weeks to come! But we couldn't give up… with lots of lessons learned, we shut for a few days and reopened with a new three-phase power supply. We were very naive and didn't realise that the anonymous clients were 'rich and famous' Norwich residents. Eventually, however, we must have done something right as we achieved a good reputation (Egon Ronay recommended) and the owners of Rolls-Royces, Jaguars, Bentleys and Lotus cars become regular customers. We had many successful evenings in the early days, including a memorable Halloween Night in 1963 when we served witch's brew (home-made vegetable soup) from a copper cauldron over the open fire in the restaurant.

Christmas food served that year impressed people so much they rebooked for the following year. We also changed the style of the menus, settling for the scroll menu – printed on linen singed at the edges. In 1967 we introduced the first microwave oven to defrost frozen food. It was the size of a small wardrobe!

Now to the famous fish tank! We always served the chosen fish from the tank and had regular top-up deliveries of fresh trout in tanks from Gloucester. Fresh lobsters came from the fishmonger in Timber Hill, Norwich. We even had locally grown asparagus in season and strawberries from a market garden in Postwick Lane. On Saturday nights, in the early days, we presented female guests with buttonholes from roses bought from Morse Roses in Brundall.

Another interesting thing, although I never witnessed it myself, was that many late-night diners related how they saw ghosts in the inglenook fireplace. This phenomenon, which was repeated over and over, was of a little old man and his wife (?) sitting and watching on each side of the fireplace. I wonder if they are still there?

In the bread oven beside the inglenook fireplace

we found a William of Orange shilling, which was identified by the curator of Strangers Hall in Norwich. She also confirmed that, built in 1540, the Old Beams was the original White Horse pub in Brundall. We showed her the lack of foundation to the building – it sits on a sand base. During the construction, the beams were assembled in kit form (matched by scratched Roman numerals on the upstairs beams). I hope you can still see them.

We sold up in 1971.

I think the late-night cards sessions before 1971 were true. In fact, one of the card players, John North, a good customer from the oil rig suppliers, became the next owner of the Old Beams. Between 1972 and 2002 I believe the restaurant changed hands several times.

Famous visitors at that time included Cliff Richard, Clement Freud, Pete Murray, Colin Chapman of Lotus cars, Harry Corbett and Ron Saunders, then manager of Norwich City.

Incidentally, many souvenirs must be around in Norfolk. We lost all the linen scroll menus, all the horse brasses and the little vases for fresh flowers in the first year!

Manor Garage, the Manor House and St Ninians
Barbara Ayers

The earliest owner traced is Richard Baldwin, a farmer, who died in 1725, and you can see his initials on the eastern gable of the house, which was only ever a manor house in name. In 1909 G.S. Hotblack owned what is now the Manor House, together with Manor Garage and the land on which St Ninians stands. In that year he sold the land for £175 to Dr Robert McKelvie to build St Ninians on. In 1967 Michael Harrison bought St Ninians from Ernest Parker, owner of the Norvic shoe company. The Harrison family lived there for 35 years.

In the January 1916 edition of the *Blofield Deanery Magazine* there is a reference to Mr Hotblack's barn being used for intercessions for Braydeston Church.

In 1922 the Manor House and barn were sold by Hotblack's executors for £725 to a Mr Stephens. At the time W.J. Blake was a tenant, and his son, who was later to become Lord Blake, was born in the house. George E. Stephens is entered in the 1925 edition of *Kelly's Directory* as a motor engineer. According to Wesley Key's diary, 'It was a haulage contractors more than a garage.' From 1930 the house and garage were owned by Richard Cole, and it only later that they became separate properties.

From 1946 to 1957 Colonel Dicker lived in the house before swapping houses with the Backs (of Backs Wines), who lived in Springfield in Station New Road.

Meanwhile, according to Wesley Key, who later owned Strumpshaw Hall Steam Museum:

The Manor House.

St Ninians, Strumpshaw Road, 1923.

After getting the pigs sold I met the owner of a garage in Brundall and went to the pictures with him one night. He told me he was on the verge of bankruptcy. When he told me how much his debts were I told him I would pay his debts and take half the business over with him. I ran it for two years and bought him out and sold it at a fair price.

As for the pigs: 'At that time pigs were very cheap and I couldn't sell them fat so I had two killed and sold them, which showed me a profit of 30s. each.'

Wesley, according to his diary, bought Richard Cole out in 1935 and sold to a Mr Wilson in 1937. According to *Kelly's Directory*, R.S. Cole was a qualified steam, motor, mechanical and electrical engineer

Manor Garage. Left to right: Ivan Forster, Billy Tidman, Ellen Dunne, Roy Howlett.

Manor Garage, 1936. ?, ?, Wesley Key, Bill Tidman.

and funeral furnisher. Billy Tidman, who many people remember in association with the Manor Garage, worked for Stephens, Cole, Key & Wilson. After the war Billy Tidman became manager and eventually bought the business. He provided a taxi service and was also a special constable. He retired in 1989 aged 77.

Brundall Library
Wendy Ward

It was in 1935 that Miss Corder of Corder House in The Street suggested to Mr Pay that a collection of books should be organised for Brundall. Mr Pay (Fred) and his wife Winnie had moved to Brundall in 1934, shortly after their marriage, and he worked in the treasurer's department of the County Council. He approached the County Library and was asked by Miss Newberry if he could find a room and a lock-up for the books. The annexe to Brundall House, next to Pendle Cottage, was offered by Mr Finch, and Mr Sage, who lived above the annexe, opened the room up when required. There was an electric fire and a tin box in which to keep the books. Both Miss Newberry and Miss Prothero, along with two girls from the staff, came to change all the book stock on Thursday afternoons three times a year. In 1940, when the Army commandeered Brundall House, Revd Chamberlin, the rector, offered the use of the Church Room. Situated behind Oaklands, in The Street, which was formerly a farmhouse, it is thought that the Church Room was originally a barn, part of the property. With a thatched roof, this rectangular room, with a platform at the far end, was heated by an ancient 'tortoise' stove, which constantly belched forth fumes. In 1900 the room was being used as a Primitive Methodist Mission Hall and in 1908 is listed as a Mission Hall with a Sunday school and working men's club. After this it was also used by the Girls' Friendly Society and for concerts and whist drives. After the end of the Second World War Mr Church was the rector, but Mr Chamberlin, who still owned the Church Room, decided that he didn't want the library to be housed there any longer – he thought the Memorial Hall was more suitable. However, the management committee of the Memorial Hall decided that they did not want the library housed there either. Mr Pay suggested to the County Library that they should buy the Church Room, which they duly did. For many years the quarter acre of land behind the building has been rented to a local householder whose property adjoins it, but it is occasionally used during the summer months for story hours with very young children.

To make the building more suitable for use, a vestibule was installed with a new front door. Mr Walker of Shiels Court gave some furniture – shelves, a desk, a table and two chairs. There were 300 books in all, children's books being housed at the far end of the room on the raised platform. The library is not in the best position in the village – a narrow path, about 60 yards long, leads from The Street to the building – and book exchanges were made using a wheelbarrow and the trolley which Mr Pay used for his bees! To make matters worse, no signs were allowed on The Street indicating the position of the library so all 250 houses in the village were supplied with this information. The library opened on Tuesdays and Thursdays from 2.30 to 4.00 in the afternoons and from 6.30 to 8.00 in the evenings.

After the war Mrs Pay joined her husband as a volunteer at the library centre, and during the colder parts of the year could be seen arriving early to light the coke 'tortoise' stove. The population of Brundall at this time was about 990, of whom 205 were registered readers, and 5,196 books were issued. By 1971 the population had risen to 2,574, but no statistics are available as to the number of readers and books.

Under local government reorganisation in April 1974 the county was divided into four divisions based on Norwich, Great Yarmouth, Kings Lynn and County Hall, and the decision was finally made that Brundall centre was big enough to become a part-time branch library. Mr Pay had died in 1972, having given 37 years service to the village centre, and Mrs Pay had reached retirement age. Reluctantly she had to relinquish the care of her beloved books, but the library did need a cleaner and Winnie asked to be

Wendy Ward with the library exchange van she drove to Brundall Library in the mid- to late '50s.

*Daphne ffiske on Billy
Stone's horse at Hillside.*

house and did all the baking, etc., and could often be seen riding her 'sit up and beg' bike along The Street. Miss Lyla worked in Norwich, very much the business lady, but she did keep rabbits, both as pets and for the table. I used to collect dandelions and hogweed for the rabbits and, with my aunt, looked after them when the family took their annual holidays to Lowestoft. Mr Page had one of the first telephones in Brundall and I loved to be allowed into his library, so that I could pick up the receiver and ask for a line so he could make a call! When Mr Page wanted to go to Norwich on business, he would telephone for Bert Pattle to come to pick him up in his taxi. I also enjoyed doing jigsaws with him in this room. We did not have any pictures to help us put the pieces together, as Mr Page would have a picture he liked mounted on wood and then hand cut. I still have a couple of them which he gave me! Miss Lyla collected stamps and had a vast collection. She also encouraged me to start one of my own. Miss Fan introduced me to coffee, made with hot milk (which I hated), boiled on the Valor oil-burning range in the kitchen. I used to run errands on a Saturday for her, and my reward was usually coffee, a freshly baked scone and 6d! I only drink black coffee now! Mr Page grew asparagus and figs, neither of which I had seen growing anywhere else. I loved eating the fresh figs and once got told off for cutting some asparagus fern to put in with a bunch of sweet peas I had gathered!

The Pages were always very supportive of Blofield and District Silver Band, as were the Lings, who were to occupy Braydescroft later. The band held their AGMs at Braydescroft and always made sure they included the house when they played carols round the village at Christmas. They would play in the hall and then be given seasonal refreshments.

Hillside, Station New Road
Paul Ingram, Jackie Biss

Built at the beginning of the twentieth century, before 1911, deeds traced back to 1845 show that Hillside was built on land which had been used for arable purposes. One of the owners in the late 1800s was Sir Reginald Beauchamp of Langley Park, Loddon. Deeds dating from 1882 show land sold to the Great Eastern Railway Co. 'for the purpose of their proposed railway from Brundall to Acle and Yarmouth'. The Hillside land was part of rented out arable and pasture land known as 'The Ten Acres'.

Marion Marshall sold the house to Alexander Eddington in 1911. It was sold to Charles Bexford-Hill in 1914 and to Geoffrey ffiske in 1917. Mr ffiske moved into Hillside in 1917 with his wife, Ethel Mary Dandridge, after their marriage. It was then a three-storey thatched building. In the late 1930s, when the thatch burned and the building was razed to the first storey, it was rebuilt with a tiled roof. The ffiskes' handyman and cleaner (husband and wife) lived across the road in the old thatched cottage at No. 15 Strumpshaw Road. The cricket field area used to be rented out by the ffiskes to the Gravers of Blossom Hill Nurseries.

Mr and Mrs Biss moved into Hillside in 1970 and planted many of the existing trees and hedges. The distinctive tree within the boundary of the cricket ground is an ash tree. They also bought land on the southern side of what was then their boundary and incorporated a small carp lake within it. Later they purchased land from British Rail which includes part of the public footpath. The land stretches from the lake to Brundall's main railway station.

The Maples, The Street
Helen and Janet Etheridge

As with much of the land in Brundall, the plot on which The Maples now stands was once part of Tuck's Strumpshaw Hall estate. After his death the land was eventually bought by Fleming Hewitt, Esq, of Gorleston, in 1882. Despite being 224th on the Royal Hotel auction list, Mr Hewitt persevered to purchase land amounting to '1 acre, 3 roods and 3 perches'. He did not stay long, for in 1886 the house was bought by J. Ayris, a Norwich civil engineer. Until this point the property was used probably as a smallholding, providing a second income for the owners. The 'dwelling house' was on the same spot as the house is now, but comparatively smaller, and maps show that there were several agricultural buildings surrounding the house, including the barns today known as 'Barn Row'. There was also a substantial orchard behind the buildings.

However, all this was to change in 1889, when the house was sold to Mathew Bane Stockings. Mr Stockings, a grocer and tea merchant, ran his own shop, Stockings & Son, on St Stephen's Street, Norwich. It is clear that he didn't buy the house to live in himself, as he is shown on the 1901 census to be residing at 'No 1, The Crescent' – a prestigious address, still standing off Chapelfield Road. The house was probably an investment and Mr Stockings improved the building so considerably that there is now very little trace of the basic 'dwelling-house' that was there before. He laid out pleasant gardens and a carriage driveway and made it the house it is today. With Brundall by then a popular place for the middle classes to live, he rented it out.

One family to live in The Maples during this time was the Sennitt family. Unfortunately, their son, Claude Cushing Sennitt, died in 1917 fighting at the front during the First World War. Another occupant of The Maples also died in tragic circumstances. In 1933 the then owner of the house, William Shave, a bank manager, died on the road to Norwich. He had only gone out to do some shopping!

Surely the most charming story about this house has to be that of the signatures found on the wallpaper in the third bedroom. Whilst decorating this room, the current occupants discovered a drawing with the signature of a Mr Chapman, dated 1894. He was probably a tenant, as this was during the time that Mr Stockings owned the house.

Subsequent owners have signed their names and then repapered the wall. Coincidentally, three of these subsequent owners have been solicitors. Gilbert William Daynes, who bought the house in 1919, was a partner in Daynes, Chittock & Back. He was also a Mason and wrote books on the history of the society, including *Untrodden Paths of Masonic Research*. Jonathan Morgan, who lived at The Maples from 1971 to 1996, was another solicitor, as is the 2007 owner, Richard Etheridge.

The Maples is a wonderful example of a house that has evolved with the village. From being used for agricultural purposes by the main local landowner, it became a smallholding after Tuck's death, which meant that his estate was broken up, and then became a large and comfortable middle-class home, suitable for the type of people that Brundall appealed to at the turn of the last century – professionals who possibly came one day to visit Brundall Gardens and decided to make The Maples their home.

Starting to Research the History of Your House
Helen Etheridge

The very first place you should start when researching the history of your house is with the deeds for the property. Now mortgage companies don't need to keep them any more, everyone should have access to these. Although they may be written in technical and legal language, they can provide you with a lot of details, such as the names of the owners (although not necessarily of the occupants, because in the past more people rented than owned homes), the amount they paid, their occupations, and the dates when the property changed hands.

Armed with this information there are two places that should be top of your list to visit; the Heritage Centre in The Forum, Norwich and Norfolk Record Centre, at County Hall. Both have a whole host of resources that can help you.

If anyone remarkable has lived in your house it is an idea to have a look at the newspaper archives, which, for some newspapers, go back to the early-eighteenth century. These can be accessed at the Heritage Centre and are very easy to look at. Here you can also view Picture Norfolk, a computerised archive of old photographs of Norfolk. If you search by area you may find a picture of your home on here. Remember to ask the staff if they have any more photographs or postcards in the store rooms, which haven't been computerised yet. Staff can also search for sales details for the property. Do remember that your house may not always have had the same name as it has today, so this could lead to some dead ends. If your house was one of the larger or more interesting properties in the area, the chances are it will feature in *Kelly's Directory*, first published in the nineteenth century and continuing into the twentieth. The Heritage Centre has some reference copies of the directory to view.

The Archive Centre also has copies to look at, as well as maps, manorial records and many varied documents about your area. It is interesting to just go and have a look through the records to do with your area and see if you can discover anything interesting.

For the kind of details that you won't find in documents, neighbours who have lived in the area for a long time can provide invaluable help.

Happy house-history hunting!

CHAPTER 9

Six Thousand Years and More to Come
This Lovely Village Has Been Home

A Cycle Ride through the Village
Barbara Ayers

In 1899 some visitors arrived looking for Brundall Gardens:

It was a day in the merry month of May when we arrived at Brundall Station, on exploration bent. A solemn-faced countryman, of whom we enquired of our destination, stood still for a minute or two until the exact meaning of our interrogation dawned upon him, and he was certain that there was no ulterior motive behind it, and then he drawled out in an exasperatingly deliberate fashion, 'The gardens you want is fudder down the road. You kape on 'till you come to a gate; that's where 'tis.' And it was.

You may not meet this gentleman, but leave the car at home today and cycle, or walk if you prefer, through the village with me and you will meet others, if only in your imagination! See the village through the eyes of those who remember how it used to be. Imagine

Barbara Ayers, 2007.

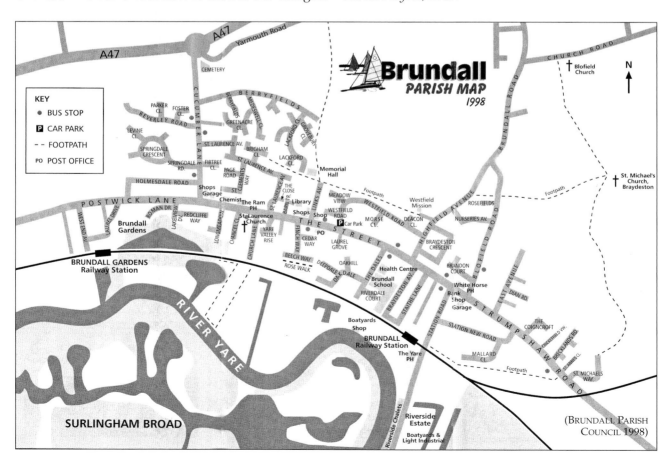

Horse chalets in the garden. In many old photos there is a pond on the corner of Blofield Road. This was possibly used for steam vehicles originally but later was welcome refreshment for passing cattle. After George left the White Horse the 'Pavilion' burnt down in 1973 and then, after changing hands several times, both trade and the building eventually went into decline and, sadly it was demolished in 2001 and replaced by five houses.

The Street
The main road has now become The Street. If you look upwards you can sometimes see interesting things otherwise missed, such as weather vanes – there is one of an old car and petrol pump on the roof of Manor Garage.

In 1967 Geoffrey ffiske wrote to George Levine: 'Great controversy about Telephone coming to village (in 1898) – many objected to wires and posts – eventually agreed if posts were decorated with finials.' There are still one or two of these left. Feelings ran high and in the 1960s Parish Council meetings were packed when street lighting was discussed. 'Rural-minded inhabitants outvoted urban newcomers, who missed their sodium lights,' wrote Geoffrey ffiske to the *Eastern Daily Press*.

Before Elliots, the estate agents, was on the corner, Barclays Bank was there. It closed in 2000 in spite of much protest.

Barclays Bank established a presence in 1964, building a 'shed' on the White Horse car park.

Merrisons' shop and Post Office, 1908.

Merrisons Shop and Post Office
Originally there was just the building on the corner and it was Merrisons shop and Post Office. Harriet Merrison had it built and gave it to her son, Charles, who ran it with his wife, Edith:

Charlie, Mr Merrison, would weigh out such items as sugar, butter, cheese, biscuits, etc., all into blue 'sugar paper' or brown-paper bags and greaseproof paper, and put everything in your basket for you, or sometimes a brown, thick paper carrier bag if you had too much for the basket. There was no self-service and everything was entered into an account book, the bill being settled at the end of the week.

We didn't have a telephone at home and to make a call I had to go to the kiosk outside Merrison's shop, lift the receiver and ask the operator for 'trunks'. She would then ask me to insert 2s. or half a crown, dial the number I had given her and if the person answered I had to press button A to go ahead with the call. If no reply, it was press button B for the money to be returned.

The Merrisons had two daughters, Elizabeth and Brenda. Brenda remembers delivering telegrams on her bicycle right through to Buckenham and Strumpshaw and all around, as well as in Brundall. Because it was during the war the news wasn't always good. Her father died at an early age and Brenda's mother ran the shop until 1962, when she sold the business to Frederick and Joyce Beck.

Becks
Before it was taken over by the Becks, the Post Office went to the Naylors for a short time and then to the Taylors. The Becks built the single-storey extension for themselves and Tacon's, the electricians. They added some self-service aisles and also delivered

From left to right: *Frederick and Joyce Beck outside their shop with Sheila Ashford and Mr Everett.*

Sally and Laurence Leeder prepare the daily newspaper delivery.

An early view of Highfield Avenue looking towards The Street.

Highfield Avenue in 1915, looking towards Blofield.

groceries to the boatyards for holidaymakers hiring out the cruisers. In about 1965 it became a Spar shop, still under the management of the Becks. When it eventually became Barclays Bank they didn't need the extension, so Tacons moved into the middle shop. The shop they vacated has been a small supermarket and at the time of writing is a fish and chip shop.

Frederick and Joyce's daughter, Sally, married Laurence Leeder, and both Sally and Laurence are familiar to the residents of Brundall as they deliver newspapers in their trademark Landrovers.

Common Lane
Glance down Station Road and you will see where Cotman painted a view of Common Lane, as it was called then. If we go down Station Road and across the level crossing we come to The Yare public house.

The Yare
On the 1881 census it was called Bleak House and belonged to William Skipper, a solicitor. In 1888 it became The Yare Hotel. For a short time in the '70s it was called The Queen Elizabeth but soon reverted back to being The Yare.

The Avenue
Angela Rowles remembers Highfield Avenue:

I first came to live in Brundall in the 1950s, but I had visited the village many times before that, as my grandfather and aunts, uncles and cousins all lived in either Highfield Avenue or East Avenue. The earliest photographs of me were taken when I was only a few months old in the orchard of my grandfather's bungalow, shortly after the end of the Second World War.

Highfield Avenue was a very rutted, unmade, tree-lined road, very muddy in winter, dusty in summer. At the top end, adjoining The Street, was a smallholding belonging to George Smith and his family. I remember being friends with his daughter, Jennifer. There was a fruit orchard along the boundary with the avenue, which was all cleared when the land was sold to Hacketts the builders in the early 1960s. Further down the avenue stood my grandfather's bungalow, which has

since been demolished, and the property which was then built on the land has since been replaced too. We entered the garden through a gate under an arch – it seemed like the 'secret garden' – and, as well as the orchard, grandfather had a very productive kitchen garden and he also kept hens.

The Royal Observer Corps
Chris Basey writes about the Royal Observer Corps post, which could be reached via Highfield Avenue:

Midway along the footpath which runs from Long's Loke (now Links Avenue) to the Westfield Mission, on the old golf links at Brundall, stood 'The Post'. It was just by a field gate into Henry Morse & Sons' rose field, known as 'Barn Field', and convenient for the telephone wires which ran along the boundary hedge.

This was where the members of the local crew of the Royal Observer Corps carried out their wartime duties from soon after the outbreak of war.

The Brundall 'Post', known by the call sign 'Victor Two', was a wooden box-like structure about 10 feet square, standing on iron legs and open to the sky. It had an adjoining covered lean-to for shelter, with facilities for rest and a coke cooking stove. Most ROC posts were at ground level, but at Brundall the additional height was needed for greater visibility over the Yare valley to the south.

Royal Observer Corps, Brundal,l 1939–45. Left to right, back row: *Charlie Hodds, Frank Platten, Nigel Johnson, Neville Langridge, Bert Platten, Albert Greenacre, Jack Paul;* middle row: *Barney Broom, Mr Enoch, Betty Read, Morris, Hettie Mitchell, Miriam Basey, Frank Platten, Wolfendale, Colin Wood;* front row: *Gordon Johnson, Clifford Ford, Charlie Merrison, J. Reeve, Stanley Mitchel, ?, Lewis Edwards.*

The 'Post' had what was referred to as 'The Post Instrument', which enabled the crew to determine the height and distance of aircraft. That information was transmitted to the group by using a 'head and breast' telephone.

Next to the post stood a shed, a chemical toilet and (after 1943) a GL radar shack. Shrouded in secrecy at the time, this was used in the detection of enemy aircraft when they infiltrated the groups of returning British bombers. Its diesel generator was maintained on 12-hour shifts by two members of the Royal Air Force, who lodged with the Simpson family on Blofield Road.

The post's crew soon increased to about 30 people, who provided two observers for round-the-clock shifts. Full-timers did eight hours and part-timers usually did four-hour duties.

At first Observers had no uniform – just a navy-blue beret with an Observer Corps badge, a steel helmet, a respirator and a police blue and white armband over-printed in red with the words 'Observer Corps'. Later, they were issued with the blue RAF-type trousers and battle-dress blouse which carried an embroidered ROC badge on the left breast.

They had to be skilled in the use of the phonetic alphabet, and with the Vocabulary of Aircraft Movement as used throughout the Armed Forces. Their aircraft recognition had to be of a very high standard in order to pass accurate information to the Norwich Headquarters to be used by the Royal Air Force as well as the Anti-aircraft gunners (Ack-Ack).

Local lads, too, were familiar with the many manuals, pamphlets and sets of cards on aircraft recognition – both friendly and enemy. There was great competition to correctly identify Spitfires, Hurricanes, Blenheims and Fairey Battles, as well as the German Messerschmitt 109s, Dorniers and Heinkels. Comics published identification puzzles which showed just part of an aeroplane, such as a rear turret, an engine shape or a tail plane, from which the aircraft had to be identified.

The men and women in the crew of the Brundall post came from all walks of life. Charlie Hodds lived by the river and was a boatyard worker. Mr Langridge farmed at Postwick – part of his farm is now the 'park and ride'. Albert Greenacre was able to regale his colleagues with tales of 'Greenacre of The Yard'. Barney Broom ran Broom's Boatyard with his brother Basil, and Mr Enoch was an agricultural merchant at Lingwood Granary. Husband and wife Stanley and Hettie Mitchell fitted in their duties with his tailoring business and boating on the river. Of the other ladies, Miss Read was from the Cucumber Lane Nursery family, Miss Morris was the daughter of Dr Morris, who was in charge of Little Plumstead Hospital, and Miriam Basey cared for her parents in Highfield Avenue.

Perhaps the youngest member of the crew was Frank Platten, who worked at Long's butcher's shop until he was called up to the Royal Air Force. His father, Bert, a full time Observer, worked at a boatyard and, during the First World War, had been awarded the Distinguished Conduct Medal with the Suffolk Regiment. Another First World War veteran was Mr Wolvendale, who sported the wings and large moustache of the Royal Flying Corps. He was the local school dentist and towed his caravan/surgery to park on school playgrounds. Jack Paul, of Boulton & Paul, lived at Riverscourt.

pensioners, whom she regularly visited, and for many years she was a churchwarden of Brundall Church. Following her death her friends set up a memorial fund and decided to erect a plaque on the tree, of which she was very fond. The bronze plaque, in an oak frame, carries the inscription 'Margery Palmer's Oak. "By works was faith made perfect.". 1889–1970. A tribute from family and friends.' The quotation was chosen by Revd Geoffrey Church, a former rector of Brundall Church, and was taken from the Epistle of St James, Chapter 2, Verse 22. Unfortunately, during the summer of 1970, before the plaque was erected, the tree was struck by lightning and suffered severe damage. At first it was feared it would have to be felled, but advice was taken and it was decided to try and save it with extensive tree surgery. Peter Jamieson, whose parents lived next door, was studying at the Royal Academy of Art and had done a drawing of the cottage. He decided to make a woodcut of this, enabling a limited number of prints to be sold so that the work of saving the tree could be paid for. Everyone was delighted when the tree burst into leaf the following spring.

Wilby Cottage.
(PRINT FROM WOODCUT BY PETER JAMIESON)

in her little car, called Henrietta!

When I was 16 my parents decided to move to St Ninian's, but they didn't sell No. 3 Holmesdale Road (which has since been renumbered 45). My grandfather lived there when he decided to leave Norwich after my grandmother died, and then my aunt and uncle from Canada moved there when they retired in 1968. I lived at St Ninian's until I got married, when, by a curious coincidence, I went to live at No. 3 Holmesdale Road. It wasn't the same house of course, the address was the other end of the road because of the renumbering.

Holmesdale Road

We will now go down Holmesdale Road, one end of which is in Postwick Lane and the other in Cucumber Lane. Golda Conneely writes:

My father, Michael Harrison, was left No. 3 Holmesdale Road by his widowed aunt, Violet E. Ward, so when he and my mother, Elizabeth Wilkinson, decided to get married in 1949 they were very happy to move into a three-bedroomed bungalow. My mother had lived in Brundall since the early 1930s, first at Field House, then at Grovelands on Postwick Lane. When I was born in 1950, Holmesdale Road was not made up, and there were no houses on the other side of the road, just a wide strip of land which most people used to grow vegetables, or to park a car. It seemed strange that the garage which had been built next to the house was really too small for a car – did that mean that cars were much smaller before the 1950s? The only way to put the car away was for my father to position it very carefully and then push it in from behind. With the aid of several pieces of wood the car was guided correctly and stopped in the right place. Getting it out again was rather risky, as it had to be pulled backwards, of course.

My great-aunt and my grandmother lived at Grovelands, on Postwick Lane, and we used to go there for baths when I was very small – there was no bath in our house, just the usual zinc tub. I recall sitting on my mother's knee wrapped in a towel as she drove us home

The District Nurse's House

No. 20 Cucumber Lane has a plaque on it which reads, 'District Nurse, Norfolk County Council, 1962'. At that time the doctors' surgery was at Bradesfield on Blofield Road. The district nurse was a nurse in her own right and had very little contact with the surgery. She had her own house and people would refer themselves to her there. She did much of the basic nursing, such as bathing, while the actual medical nursing, such as applying dressings, was left to the doctors.

Bellenden

There is a bungalow on the corner of Cucumber Lane (formerly Brundall Lane) and St Laurence Avenue that belonged to the Read family. It is called Bellenden after a place in Australia. During the First World War Henry Read met an Australian nurse who came from there, and he promised her that if he survived his wounds and ever had a place of his own that is what he would call it.

Berryfields

The land where Berryfields is now was originally part of the estate of Brundall House, then became land belonging to Manor Farm, which belonged to May Read's father.

In the 1970s the land making up Berryfields was taken over by R&J.M. Place of Tunstead and was given over to the growing of raspberries and strawberries. Fruit picking was a major feature in Brundall for a short time each summer. It provided casual employment for local people and for those from neighbouring areas, who arrived by bus at the top of Cucumber Lane.

On a warm summer's evening the sweet smell of raspberries and strawberries would have filled the air.

a) Brundall Post Office, c.1914.

b) The White Horse, 1935.

c) Outside Brundall House, 1914.

d) Outside Brundall House during the First World War.

e) The Street looking east (the present-day supermarket is on the right).

f) The Street looking west, 1913.

g) Outside the Maples, 1911.

Postcards of Brundall Street. A popular method of keeping in touch in the early-twentieth century, postcards now provide an invaluable record of our village.

CHAPTER 10

We Hold it Dear, Remember Well
Our Lives Spent in Burn-in-the-Dell

Memories
Barbara Ayers

We've read books, interviewed countless people, made phone calls, written letters and emails and received replies both from all over the UK and from abroad. We've consulted the internet, pored over old maps and documents and visited museums, the Archive Centre, the library and the Family History Centre in Norwich. We've taken photographs, talked to people, read Parish Council minutes, perused old newspapers and much, much more to bring you *The Book of Brundall and Braydeston*.

We've learnt about people and places and we know about events and when they happened. The nearest we can get, however, to experiencing for ourselves the sights and sounds, and even the smells and tastes, of yesteryear, is to read the memories of people who lived through those times, and we include some of the more evocative of them here. Of course, in 2007 many of the childhood memories of our older inhabitants are going to involve the Second World War.

As well as a past, Brundall has a present and a future, and to reflect this we will conclude with the impressions of a rector new to the village in 2006 and of pupils from Brundall School in 2007.

'Don't You Know There's a War On?'
Chris Basey

My first memory of the Second World War in Brundall was of standing in the garden of our Highfield Avenue home early one Sunday evening and hearing, then seeing, three German planes flying low on their way to Norwich. They were so low and close that we could see the crews quite clearly and the black cross markings on the sides of the aircraft left no room for doubt that they were the enemy!

One of the worst things about the war was that we couldn't go to the seaside. We did make one visit just to see the extent of the barbed wire and iron which had been installed all along Lowestoft beach. Sadly, we had to forget the beach for another five years or so. We were not going to be deprived of messing about in the water, though, as we were so near to

Highfield Avenue fire engine, 1938.

Subscribers

Carolyn Abbott, Angels Beauty Salon, Brundall

John and Joan Adams, Brundall, Norfolk

Martin and Jackie Adams, Northampton

Dr Brenda Akeroyd, Granddaughter of Dr Michael Beverley

Anthea Allen, Campbell River, BC, Canada

David Allison, Thorpe St Andrew, Norwich

Mrs Doreen P. Andrews, Brundall, Norfolk

Roger B. Andrews, Brundall, Norfolk

Sheila Ashford, Strumpshaw

Linda Ashwood (née Hollis), Brundall, (formerly Blofield)

Roland Ayers, Norwich, Norfolk

Barbara and Peter Ayers, Brundall, Norfolk

Emily Ayers, Greenwich, London

Monica and Tony Aylett, Brundall

Chris and Ann-Marie Baker, Brundall Gardens

Molly Baker, Brundall, Norfolk

Simon and Anne Baker, Brundall Gardens

Mr I. Baker, Brundall, Norfolk

Rachael Banham, Loddon, Norfolk

J.E. Barber, West Sussex

Jan and Peter Barrington, Brundall

Ronald J. Batchelor (deceased), Brundall

Rita M. Baxter, Holmesdale Road, Brundall

James Behagg, Attleborough

Andrew Behagg, Norwich

Lorne Betts, Brundall, Norfolk

Gerry and Rosie Bickers, Brundall

Marion R. Billham, Brundall, Norfolk

Jean Bird, Norwich, Norfolk

Carol and Michael Bishop

Mark and Michelle Blackaby, Brundall

Colin Paul Boast, Brundall, Norfolk

Victoria L. Bond, Brundall, Norfolk

Gladys Bothamley (née Barber), Braydeston

Pat Breeze, Honeywell Cottage, Honeycombe Road, Salhouse

Reginald A. Brinded, Worthing, Sussex

Derek E. Brinded, Horning, Norfolk

Keith R.G. Broom, Stalham Green

Martin and Jennifer Broom, Strumpshaw, Norfolk

Graham and Doona Broom, Christchurch, New Zealand

Emma Broom, Swannington, Norfolk

Rosemary Broom, Blakeney, North Norfolk

Simon and Kate Broom, Marlingford, Norfolk

Hamish and Madeleine Broom, Beaconsfield, Bucks

Brundall Pet and Hardware

Ian and Christine Buchanan

Sally Buckingham, Brundall

Katharine Cable, Sheffield

Mrs Margaret. H. Cable, Brundall, Norfolk

Jean and Athur Callf, Brundall

The Carding family

John and Jean Caston, Brundall, Norfolk

Denise and John Charlesworth, Desborough, Northants

Mr M.J. Cheesman, Brundall, Norfolk

Victoria, Bethany and Abigail Clarke, Brundall, Norfolk

Bob Clarke, Waen Wen, Gwynedd, North Wales

Graham and Mary Clarke, Brundall, Norfolk

Rita and Keith Clarke, Brundall

Mr & Mrs J Coles, Brundall

Michael John Cook

Julia and Aidan Coughlan, Brundall

Ivan R. Cremer, Brundall

Cyril H. Cripsey, Brundall, Norfolk

Roy and Gill Cross, Brundall

Mr John Curtis, Westfield Close, Brundall, Norwich, Norfolk

Debra A. Curtis, Brundall, Norfolk

Lyn and Paul Cutting, Brundall, Norfolk

Geraldine and David Daniel, Brundall

Peter Daniel

Andy Daniel

Allen Davis, Brundall

Mrs Suzanne Deacon, Brundall, Norfolk

Daphne Dunnett, Brundall, Norfolk

Lew and Joan Edridge, Brundall

Lewis W. Edwards, Brundall

Doris and Stan Edwards, Brundall

The Eheridge Family, Brundall

Callum D. J. Eke, Brundall, Norfolk

Simon J. Eke, Brundall, Norfolk

John M. Eke (deceased), formerly of Brundall, Norfolk

John and Sheila Evans, Saint Michaels Way, Brundall, Norfolk

Robert P. Evans, Harrison Close, Sprowston, Norwich

John Fleetwood, Parish Tree Warden

Aubrey Forster, Blofield, Norfolk

Eric Forster, Blofield, Norfolk

Mrs G. Foster, Brundall

Kath and Mike Foster, Postwick, Norwich

In Memory of Michael Freeman and 'Cadilly'

Andrew, Darren and Jeremy Fuller

Rick and Jill Fuller, Brundall

Marion, Mike, Claire and Philip Gabillia, Brundall, Norfolk

Martin B.F. Gannon

Sue and Keith Garrould, Loddon

Eileen and Graham Goldsmith, Brundall

Norman R. Gomm

Anna Gonzales (née Stubbs), Luton, Beds

M and S Goodson, Brundall

Pat Gosling, Brundall, Norfolk

Grace and Jack, Brundall

Lois Grantham

R. and P. Graver, Highfield House, Brundall

R. and P. Graver, The Gables, Brundall

Graver and Co, Brundall

Dr Ian G. Gray, now Norwich

Nicholas J. Greef, Brundall, Norfolk

Norman Green, Brundall, Norfolk

Peter and Betty Green, Brundall

Celia and Colin Green, Brundall, Norfolk

Joan Greenacre, Eye, Peterborough, Cambs

Elisabeth Greenwood, Brundall

Shirley and George Hallums, Brundall

Katherine S. Hannigan, Stafford

Edna Harman, Brundall, Norfolk

Chris and Bob Harris, Brundall, Norfolk

Tony Harris, Brundall

Ruth and Peter Harrup, Brundall

Elizabeth Hatch (née Wood), Brundall

Gerry and Celia Hawkins, Brundall, Norfolk

Dave and Barbara Hawkins, Brundall

Mr and Mrs D. Heath, Brundall

Bruce and Molly Henderson-Gray and family, Braydeston

Christine Hill and Will Hill MBE, Brundall

Barry C. and Helen F. Holdstock

Arthur (Ha'penny) Horner

Annette and Michael Horton, Brundall

Alan and Bianca Hourd, Brundall, Norfolk

Nick and Mandy Hovey, Strumpshaw, Norfolk

Chris and Anne Hussey, Brundall, Norfolk

Hutchinson family

Marie I. Illingworth, Brundall, Norfolk

Paul Ingram, Brundall, Norfolk

B. D. And M.E. Ireland, Blofield

Dulcie M. Ireland, Brundall, Norfolk

Joy James, Good Companions Club, Brundall

To Jan

Joyce Jarman, Earls Colne, Essex

Raymond and Gillian Jeckells, Horning, Norfolk

Brian (Joe) Jenkins, Brundall

Mr D.J. And Mrs A.C. Jewiss, Brundall

Jill and Jeff, Brundall

Ken and Marlene Jolly

Stephen Jolly

Jack and Olive Jonas, Brundall

Liz Jonas, Clench Warton, King's Lynn

Marion Jones, Brundall, Norfolk

Glyn and Joan Jones, Brundall

The Jones family, Brundall

Peter and Anne Keatinge, Brundall, Norfolk

Tony and Joy Kenny, Spixworth, Norwich

Mr Martyn Kenworthy, Hethersett, Norfolk

Mr Stephen Kenworthy, Blofield, Norfolk

Mr and Mrs Graham Kenworthy, Brundall

Ron and Val Kerridge, Brundall
Ruby Ruth Kerrison, Weston Cottage, Eccles on Sea, Norfolk
Catherine Kerry, Australia
Melvyn, Susan, Karys and Alys Knickle, Stilton
Colin and Jackie Lake, Brundall
Mrs M. Lamb, Strumpshaw Road
John and Glennis Larwood, Lingwood, Norfolk
Tony and Sue Larwood (née Adams), Lingwood, Norfolk
M. T. And C. Leathers, Brundall, Norfolk
John A. Ledward, Brundall, Norfolk
Teresa, Colin, Tiffany and Kiri Leman
Lianne Lewin (née Smith), Leicester
Gillian Lincoln, Brundall, Norfolk
Brenda Lincoln (née Merrison), formerly of Brundall, now Limpenhoe, Norfolk
Trevor D. Lindsell, Brundall, Norfolk
Mrs Lockwood (née Pay), High Wycombe, Bucks
Timothy J. Long, Brundall, Norfolk
Andrew and Vicki Love and family, Blofield Road, Brundall
Prof. Simon Maddrell (Grandson of Rev C.M. Chamberlin), Isle of Man
Ron Mahon and Barbara Mahon
Markwell family, Brundall, Norfolk
George Marriott, Brundall
Rory Marsden, Brundall, Norfolk
Margaret and Roger Marshall, Brundall
Brian and Florence Marshall, Brundall
D.L. Mayes, Blofield, Norfolk
Lynda and Terry Mayo, Brundall
Michael and Pauline McManus, T.I.B.
Sharon Meldrum, Burton Joyce, Notts
Mary Mills, Brundall
Allan G. Mitchell, Zurich, Switzerland
Anne Murphy, Brundall, Norfolk
Garry and Janet Muter, Brundall Gardens
Christine Neate (née Allison), Formerly of Thorpe, Norwich
Margaret and William Newsome
Mrs Patricia North, Brundall, Norfolk
Mike and Lyn Odell, Brundall, Norfolk
John Olorenshaw, Norwich, Norfolk
Mr and Mrs B.J. Owen, Brundall
Jacqueline H. Palmer, London
Ann and Ray Palmer, Brundall, Norfolk
Marie and Jack Palmer, Brundall
Mr D.A. Parke, Thorpe, Norwich
Lesley Parker, Brundall, Norfolk
Stephen Parkin, Brundall, Norfolk
Fred and Anne Parsley, Blofield, Norwich
Roger Parsons, Brundall, Norfolk
Paul Payne, Postwick, Norfolk
Mrs Daphne Peachment, Brundall, Norfolk
Kim and Andrew Pearson, Brundall
David J. Penny, Brundall, Norfolk
Maureen Philp, Brundall, Norfolk
Barbara and David Pilch, Blofield
Mrs Pummell, Brundall, Norfolk
Pauline Punt (née Hollis), formerly Blofield and Brundall
Miriam Read, Brundall, Norfolk
Mandy and Brian Read, Thurlton

Nicola Remnant (née Warnes), Blofield Heath, Norfolk (grew up in Brundall)
Amanda, Alan, Samuel and Emily Rix, Brundall, Norfolk
Eve Roberts and Rosalind Harwood, Brundall, Norfolk
Trevor F. Rose, Brundall, Norfolk
Paul and Angela Rowles (née Clarke), Tarporley, Cheshire
Clive and Gillian Royal, Brundall
Brian and Claire Russell, Brundall
Valerie Ryall (née Ward), Aston Clinton, Bucks
John and Wendy Saville
Mary and Tim Scarffe, Hemstead
Paul Scotter, Brundall, Norfolk
Angela Sellers, Brundall, Norfolk
Sendall family, Brundall
Roger and Susan Shaw, York
Wyn and Alan Sherwood, Brundall
Mrs M. Shingles, Brundall, Norwich, Norfolk
Frederick H. Short, Brundall, Norfolk
Tony and Linda Shorthose, Brundall, Norfolk
Sillitoe, Brundall, Norwich
Sinclair and Ann-Marie Simpson
Trevor and Shirley Smith, Lingwood, Norfolk
Daniel Smith, Norwich
Mr Jasper Smith, Brundall, Norfolk
Paul and Mavis Smith, Brundall, Norwich
Jenny Snook, Brundall
Stephen and Debora Snowling, Brundall
Michael. D. Snowling, Brundall
Ronald E. Spalding, Brundall
Tanya Spreadbury, Horsham 2007
Peter Spring, Brundall, Norfolk
Springdale Care Home
Elizabeth Stableford, Brundall, Norfolk
John Anthony Stableford, Brundall, Norfolk
Norma Stanforth, Brundall
Mr G.W. Stapleton, Brundall, Norfolk
Bob and Beverley Stevenson, Brundall
J.F. Stone, Lingwood (born in Brundall)
The Strowger Family, Brundall
Alison Stuart, Egham, Surrey
Fred and Doreen Stubbs, Brundall, Norfolk
Mark Stubbs, Luton, Beds
Anita Sturgess, Brundall
Chippy and Julie Summers, Brundall Gardens
David and Elrita Sykes, Pietermaritsburg, Rep. South Africa
Mabel Sykes, Brundall, Norfolk
Philip Sykes, Motueka, New Zealand
Gwen and John Talbot, Brundall
Kenneth and Barbara Taylor, Strumpshaw
Adrian and Moina Thomas, Brundall Gardens
Claire and Glyndwr Thomas, Toft Monks, Brundall Gardens
Barbara and Colin Thomas, Brundall
Sarah Jane Thomson
Kathryn Thomson
John and Jean Thomson, Brundall

The Thorneloe family, Formerly of Brundall
John and Sue Tibbenham, Brundall
Jillian Tidman, Thorpe St Andrew, Norfolk
Janet Todman, Blofield, Norwich, Norfolk
John N. W. Tripp
Maureen and John Tubby, Brundall
Susen Turner, South Walsham
Les Turnham, Welwyn Garden City
Jessica Tye-Leech, Brundall
Chris and Jenny Unsworth, Brundall, Norfolk
Judith A. Varvel, Brundall
David A. Varvel, Brundall
Dr Narinder K. Verma, Brundall, Norfolk
John F.W. Walling, Newton Abbot, Devon
Ian and Ann Walters, Brundall, Norfolk
Peter Ward, Berkhampstead
Wendy Ward, Brundall, Norfolk
Meg R. Ward, Brundall, Norfolk
Robert Ward, London
Gavin Warnes, New Jersey, USA (grew up in Brundall)
Heather and Michael Warwick
Hannah and Matthew Warwick
Mr and Mrs Roger Waterton, Brundall, Norfolk
John and Sheila Watson, Brundall
Peter and Jean Watson, Lowestoft
Stanley and Vivienne Weavers
The Dixon/Webster Family, Formerly of Barn Terrace
Mr and Mrs Simon. Welin, Brundall, Norwich
Dr W.G. and Mrs D. Wenley, formerly of Brundall
Jean A. Whiley, Brundall, Norfolk
Sandra and David Whiting, Brundall
Brenda and John Whittaker, Brundall
Kevin J. Whittaker, Brundall, Norfolk
Josephine A. Wightman
Sylvia and Jim Wilkins
David Wilkinson, Brundall, Norfolk
Tim Wilkinson, West Harrow, Middx
Mrs B.K. Willgress, Acle, Norwich
Debbie Williams, Brundall
E.C. Williams, Norfolk
Williams family, Brundall, Norfolk
Anne-Marie Wilson, Brundall, Norfolk
The Wiltshire family, Brundall
Ian and Lesley Witard, Brundall
Christopher C. Wood, Brundall
Louis W.G. Wood, Brundall
Martyn L. Wood, Brundall
Peter D. Wood, Lingwood
Steven Woodhouse, Brundall, Norfolk
David and Alice Woolston, Brundall, Norfolk
Tim J. Worrall, Wolverhampton, West Midlands
Matthew Wright, Brundall
Elizabeth and Derek Wright, Brundall
Louise Wright, Brundall
The Yare Public House
Chris Yeates, Norwich
Sarah Yeates, Brundall
David and Jane Yeates, Brundall